MULTIFORM

ARCHITECTURE
IN AN AGE OF
TRANSITION

T0385443

AD

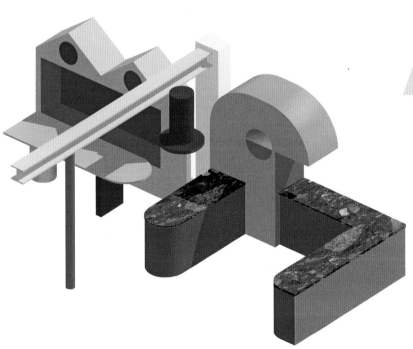

Guest-edited by
OWEN HOPKINS and
ERIN MCKELLAR

01 | Vol 91 | 2021

ISSN 0003-8504
ISBN 978 1119 717669

Guest-edited by **Owen Hopkins and Erin McKellar**

AOC, V&A Museum of Childhood,
Bethnal Green, London,
due for completion 2022

Editorial Offices
John Wiley & Sons
9600 Garsington Road
Oxford
OX4 2DQ

T +44 (0)1865 776 868

Editor
Neil Spiller

Managing Editor
Caroline Ellerby
Caroline Ellerby Publishing

Freelance Contributing Editor
Abigail Grater

Publisher
Todd Green

Art Direction + Design
CHK Design:
Christian Küsters
Barbara Nassisi

Production Editor
Elizabeth Gongde

Prepress
Artmedia, London

Printed in the United Kingdom
by Hobbs the Printers Ltd

Front cover: Studio
MUTT, *The Architect*, 'Out
of Character', Sir John
Soane's Museum, London,
2018. © Studio MUTT,
photo French + Tye

Inside front cover: Adam
Nathaniel Furman,
Gateways, Granary Square,
London, 2017. © Gareth
Gardner

Page 1: Office S&M, Mo-tel
House, Islington, London,
2020. © Office S&M

01/2021

∆ ARCHITECTURAL DESIGN

January/February
2021

Profile No.
269

Journal Customer Services
For ordering information,
claims and any enquiry
concerning your journal
subscription please go to
www.wileycustomerhelp
.com/ask or contact your
nearest office.

Americas
E: cs-journals@wiley.com
T: +1 877 762 2974

**Europe, Middle East
and Africa**
E: cs-journals@wiley.com
T: +44 (0)1865 778315

Asia Pacific
E: cs-journals@wiley.com
T: +65 6511 8000

Japan (for Japanese-
speaking support)
E: cs-japan@wiley.com
T: +65 6511 8010

Visit our Online Customer
Help available in 7 languages
at www.wileycustomerhelp
.com/ask

Print ISSN: 0003-8504
Online ISSN: 1554-2769

Prices are for six issues
and include postage and
handling charges. Individual-
rate subscriptions must be
paid by personal cheque or
credit card. Individual-rate
subscriptions may not be
resold or used as library
copies.

All prices are subject to
change without notice.

Identification Statement
Periodicals Postage paid
at Rahway, NJ 07065.
Air freight and mailing in
the USA by Mercury Media
Processing, 1850 Elizabeth
Avenue, Suite C, Rahway,
NJ 07065, USA.

USA Postmaster
Please send address changes
to *Architectural Design*,
John Wiley & Sons Inc.,
c/o The Sheridan Press,
PO Box 465, Hanover,
PA 17331, USA

Rights and Permissions
Requests to the Publisher
should be addressed to:
Permissions Department
John Wiley & Sons Ltd
The Atrium
Southern Gate
Chichester
West Sussex PO19 8SQ
UK

F: +44 (0)1243 770 620
E: Permissions@wiley.com

Subscribe to ∆
∆ is published bimonthly
and is available to purchase
on both a subscription basis
and as individual volumes
at the following prices.

Prices
Individual copies:
£29.99 / US$45.00
Individual issues on
∆ App for iPad:
£9.99 / US$13.99
Mailing fees for print
may apply

Annual Subscription Rates
Student: £93 / US$147
print only
Personal: £146 / US$229
print and iPad access
Institutional: £346 / US$646
print or online
Institutional: £433 / US$808
combined print and online
6-issue subscription on
∆ App for iPad: £44.99 /
US$64.99

This ∆ is dedicated to the
memory of Charles Jencks,
whose ideas and enquiring
spirit remain a constant
inspiration.

New architectural movements need their precursors and prototypes. Few buildings exert as magnetic a pull on architects as Sir John Soane's Museum in London – and so it is for Multiform. The ideas behind Multiform – as opposed to the broader tendency they attempt to describe – emerged through a series of exhibitions, projects and conversations staged at the Soane by Owen Hopkins with Erin McKellar between 2017 and 2020. This issue of Δ extends from those original discussions, while bringing in new voices and pointing to new directions.

Owen Hopkins is an architectural writer, historian and curator. He is Director of the Farrell Centre at Newcastle University. Previously he was Senior Curator of Exhibitions and Education at Sir John Soane's Museum, and before that Architecture Programme Curator at the Royal Academy of Arts. His interests revolve around the connections between architecture, politics and society, the roles of style, media and technology in architectural discourse, and architecture's varying relationships to the public and popular culture. He has curated numerous exhibitions at the Soane, including, most recently, 'Langlands & Bell: Degrees of Truth' (2020), 'Eric Parry: Drawing' (2019), 'Code Builder' (with Mamou-Mani Architects), 'Out of Character' (with Studio MUTT) and 'The Return of the Past: Postmodernism in British Architecture' (all 2018) and 'Adam Nathaniel Furman: The Roman Singularity' (2017).

A frequent commentator on architecture in the press, and on radio and TV, Hopkins is the author of six books, including *Postmodern Architecture: Less is a Bore* (Phaidon, 2020), *Lost Futures: The Disappearing Architecture of Post-War Britain* (Royal Academy of Arts, 2017), *Mavericks: Breaking the Mould of British Architecture* (Royal Academy Books, 2016) and *From the Shadows: The Architecture and Afterlife of Nicholas Hawksmoor* (Reaktion Books, 2015). He is also editor of six books/series of essays. He lectures internationally and is a regular guest critic at architecture schools as well as a judge for a number of architecture awards.

Erin McKellar is Assistant Curator of Exhibitions at Sir John Soane's Museum. She is broadly interested in interior architecture, the role of women and children in architecture, the intersection of architecture and politics and the revision of Modernism to encompass regionalism and organicism. At the Soane, she is working on an exhibition with Space Popular (2021), and has previously contributed to 'All That Could Have Been: A Project by CAN and Harry Lawson' (2020), 'Soane's Light: A Study by Hélène Binet' (2019) and 'Eric Parry: Drawing' (2019), as well as the book *The Return of the Past: Conversations on Postmodernism* (Sir John Soane's Museum, 2018).

Before her current role she completed a PhD in the History of Art and Architecture at Boston University in Massachusetts, where her thesis analysed US and UK housing exhibitions during the Second World War. She has been a fellow of the Paul Mellon Centre for Studies in British Art in London, and the Clarence S Stein Institute for Urban and Landscape Studies at Cornell University in New York. Recent publications include essays in the *Journal of Design History* and in collections for Routledge and Leuven University Press.

WHAT IS MULTIFORM?

Multiform is the perpetually provisional architectural articulation of the complexities of the contemporary world. It meets today's disorder with multiplicity, variety and plurality. It is not one thing, but many things. It is less a style than a common tendency manifested in the work of a range of architects practising today. Multiform emerges from a sensibility that distrusts the urge to organise or impose order. It resists conformity in aesthetics and ideology. It rejects architecture's instrumentalisation towards external agendas, be they financial, social or political. If Multiform has a mission, it is that architecture succeeds when it is true to itself.

Multiform appears at moments of transition. It is the architectural response to the end of neoliberalism, the climate crisis, the melding of the physical and digital spheres, and the uncertainties of the post-COVID world. It dismisses the grand narrative in favour of the particular, the tactical and the opportunistic. It exists in the margins, distributed, polycentric and diffuse. It is both one thing and another, sign and signified, literal and metaphorical, medium and message, modern and postmodern, mainstream and marginal, style and sensibility. Multiform is 'Adhocism' for the 21st century.[1] It has no beginning and it has no end. It is the infinitely hybrid architecture of a multiversal age.

In an Age of Transition

'There are decades where nothing happens; and there are weeks where decades happen,' as Vladimir Ilyich Lenin probably did not say. On the morning of Monday 15 September 2008, the world woke up to news that Lehman Brothers was filing for bankruptcy. The collapse of the 150-year-old investment bank – the fourth largest in the US – marked at a stroke the end of one era and beginning of another. The cult of free markets and deregulation that had held sway since the late 1970s, and which had allowed Lehman to grow fat – and, as it turned out, sclerotic – had been broken.

Since 2008 we have been living though the death throes of that politico-economic order, variously described as neoliberalism, and the protracted birth of its unknown successor. With the lifting of the neoliberal trance, questions of ideology that had long since been answered were suddenly up for grabs. History, it transpired, had not ended. Lehman's collapse tore the very fabric of reality, out of which unspooled previously dormant grand narratives of nationalism, populism of the left and right, identity and environmental activism.

At such moments of transition, it is natural to want to cling to something that gives meaning outside of the chaos. Architecture is no exception as a discipline that has always tended to be in thrall to the grand narrative. The Modernist aversion to ornament still holds sway, even if it now manifests an aesthetic rather than an ideological proposition. Meanwhile, nostalgia for the public-sector architect, and even more so the ideological urgency of the climate 'emergency', have been used to lend moral imprimatur to previously moribund architectural ideas.

Adam Nathaniel Furman, The Democratic Monument, 2017

left: The apotheosis of Multiform. Furman reimagines the town hall as a brightly coloured composition of different styles and materials, offering a striking symbolic reflection of the stunning variety of different cultures, identities and histories that make up today's cities.

opposite: The building's interior offers space for offices, council chambers, galleries, events and ceremonies. As a place where the individual and the collective come together, the Democratic Monument illustrates the opportunities Multiform offers for reconnecting architecture to the aesthetic and cultural pluralism that marks contemporary civic life.

The headquarters of the Lehman Brothers investment bank on 6th Avenue in downtown Manhattan on 14 September 2008

The day before the longest week. At the very moment this photograph was taken the bank stood on the precipice as frantic discussions took place to try to pull it back from the brink. The rest is history – or, rather, this was the moment that 'the end of history' itself ended.

Couched in terms of architecture's power and importance, these arguments in fact betray deep anxieties about the discipline's diminishing status and agency. It is possible to make this point and still recognise the validity of the situations that have led to the formation of grand narratives and which they aspire to change. The pernicious social, economic and environmental legacies of neoliberalism, as well as the deep societal ruptures already being opened up by far-reaching technological changes – all of which have been accelerated and exacerbated by the pandemic – demand immediate action. These diagnoses are, for the most part, correct, but the treatment prescribed is fundamentally wrong.

'Crises', 'emergencies', 'existential challenges', 'unprecedented' or 'world-ending' events – the hysteria of the language is telling. The grand narrative reduces the unimaginably complex, nuanced and multifaceted to monomaniacal solutionism and ideological sloganeering. Architecture should have learnt its lesson after witnessing the damage done in the name of 'the modern', 'the new' and 'progress' in the postwar era. Postmodernism taught us that monomaniacal architecture fails on its own terms. It is a lesson that many are at risk of forgetting – but not all.

Learning from Postmodernism

Since 2008, and in some instances before, a growing band of architects have begun to re-examine, reinterpret and redeploy a range of design tactics and approaches associated with the Postmodernism of the 1970s and 1980s. This is typically manifested through expressive uses of ornament and decoration, formal reference and quotation, stylistic eclecticism, symbolism in form, material and ornament, and the bold use of colour. We call this tendency Multiform.

Postmodernism became a dirty word in the 1990s and early 2000s, as architecture retreated towards Neomodernism, and these tactics were more or less outlawed by the mainstream consensus. The exception that proved the rule was the overtly oppositional position adopted at the time by the practice FAT – an acronym for Fashion Architecture Taste.

FAT were the Banquo's ghost of Postmodernism, jovially haunting the ascetic banquet of turn-of-the-millennium architectural culture. Fittingly, FAT departed the stage before they became too 'successful'. And true to their overtly self-conscious, fine-art-influenced approach, the practice's 'death' was staged from beyond the grave (the practice having disbanded in 2013) in a special issue of the *Architects' Journal* in 2015. In those pages, FAT co-director Charles Holland remarked how 'The Death and Life of the Architect marks various ends – fictional, architectural, professional – but it also suggests new beginnings, ways to make architecture meaningful and important again.'[2]

FAT are the John the Baptists of Multiform, blazing a trail by exposing how Neomodernism had replaced moral or ideological purity with an aesthetic one. Indirectly, they reminded architectural culture of the enduring importance of their heroes Robert Venturi and Denise Scott Brown's observation that

Architects are out of the habit of looking non-judgmentally at the environment, because orthodox Modern architecture is progressive ... it is dissatisfied with existing conditions. Modern architecture has been anything but permissive: Architects have preferred to change the existing environment rather than enhance what is there ... We look backward at history and tradition to go forward, we can also look downward to go upward. And withholding judgement may be used as a tool to make later judgement more sensitive.[3]

Multiform internalises this sensibility. Common to many of the architects in this issue of ⌀ is the realisation that so much of what has passed for 'good' architecture in recent years is unerringly polite, often dull, and frequently conservative while dressed up as progressive. Multiform reveals how far contemporary architectural culture has climbed up its ivory tower, elevating itself from everyday life and the concerns of real people.

Denise Scott Brown,
The Strip,
Las Vegas,
1965

Although Robert Venturi's name is always credited before Scott Brown's (and Steven Izenour's), it was Scott Brown who actually introduced her husband to Las Vegas. Her photographs looked beyond the extraordinary to the messy vitality of the everyday, ideas that would inform the research that became *Learning from Las Vegas* (1977).

FAT,
Blue House,
London,
2002

'Adolf Loos on the inside, South Park on the outside', as the building's architect and client, FAT director Sean Griffiths, has variously described the Blue House. The building's cartoon-like qualities, utilising a range of references deployed at different scales, were conceived to communicate its function as a home and office.

FAT,
funeral wreath created for
'The Death and Life of
the Architect' special issue
of the *Architects' Journal,*
2015

FAT may be dead, but their legacy lives on in Multiform. Reworking the title of Jane Jacobs's seminal *The Death and Life of Great American Cities* (1961), the special issue of the *AJ* explored how resurrection, zombification and other forms of design afterlives are essential to forming new architectural ideas.

Adhocism for the 21st Century

One of Postmodernism's most important progenitors emerged from a similar dissatisfaction with the moribund architectural culture of its own time. *Adhocism*, as articulated by Charles Jencks and Nathan Silver in 1972, decried how 'The present environment is trending towards both extreme visual simplicity and extreme functional complexity. This double and opposite movement is eroding our emotional transaction with and comprehension of objects.'[4]

Jencks and Silver's target was the so-called 'International Style', which they saw manifested in the identikit steel-and-glass towers that appeared in cities all over the world during the 1950s and 1960s. They rejected the idea of a universal architectural language that this style appeared to pose through its application to buildings of all types, irrespective of scale, location or climate, even as wholly new typologies emerged:

> In opposition to this, adhocism makes visible the complex workings of the environment. Instead of an homogenous surface which smooths over all distinctions and difficulties, it looks to the intractable problem as the source of supreme expression. From problems, from the confrontation of diverse subsystems, it drags an art of jagged, articulated cataclysms that shouts out the problems from every corner.[5]

Here, this analysis is very much of its time: in particular, the linguistic preoccupations of the requirement that architecture speaks, or even 'shouts', in contrast to the International Style's presumed muteness, as well as the notion of a 'jagged' aesthetic in contradistinction to its 'smooth surface'. Yet ironically given its hostility to the universal, Adhocism's prescriptions transcend the historical moment and situation from which it emerged:

Meaningful articulation is the goal of adhocism. Opposed to purism and exclusivist design theories, it accepts everyone as an architect and all modes of communication, whether based on nature or culture. The ideal is to provide an environment which can be as visually rich and varied as actual urban life.[6]

It is certainly counterintuitive to be looking today at a text that railed against the perceived stylistic conformity of late-Modernism as the negation of the complexity of 1970s everyday life, given the infinitely fragmented visual and stylistic field in which architecture now operates. But there is a difference between visual disorder and a 'rich', 'articulated', 'varied' urban setting that allows for an 'experience of a higher order', as Jencks and Silver advocated. Underneath the surface the field in which architecture operates today is as highly limited, if not more so, than it was then.

Multiform is Not a Style

Architecture has become an instrument, not of itself, but of forces and interests from outside the discipline – social, political and financial. Just as Postmodernists saw Modernism as limiting stylistic expression, so the present almost-total instrumentalisation of architecture restricts the field – expressive, experiential and stylistic – in which it operates.

The result is a moribund architecture, one-dimensional, disconnected from the world, disallowing individual expression and limited in the experiences it offers. It is architecture with little capacity for creating meaning, reference, allusion, opposition or individuality. Multiform recognises that it is only by remaining explicitly non-instrumental and staying true to its own values and ideals that architecture can serve the ends for which it is so often the means: public good, social benefit and individual wellbeing.

Multiform is the inheritor of Adhocism and Postmodernism – as well as the raging stylistic competition that characterised Modernism's origins. Unlike most inheritances, this one is active rather than passive. Multiform looks to the culture of the late 1970s and 1980s through the lens of a critical nostalgia, recognising the equivalencies between that moment of release, transition and renewal, and our present one. Insofar as Multiform manifests Postmodernism's aesthetics, it does so through employing equivalent design tactics. Collage, assemblage, quoting, admixing, remixing, sampling – Multiform appropriates Postmodernism's own modes of appropriation.

Multiform is not a revival. While frequently written off by its critics as 'neo-Postmodernism', Multiform is its own thing. It is as particular to the conditions of the present as Postmodernism was to its own. If Postmodernism was the architecture of MTV, deindustrialisation and the microwave oven, Multiform is the architecture of TikTok, e-scooters, Siri,

Apollo 11 Lunar Module flying over the moon with the Earth in the background, 1969

'We choose to go to the Moon!' The almost inconceivable challenge laid down by John F Kennedy in his speech at Rice University, Houston, on 12 September 1962 was met by the decade's end (as he demanded) not by the slick spaceships imagined in sci-fi, but through the triumph of ad-hoc design figured by the unmistakable form of the Apollo Lunar Module.

Studio MUTT,
Multi-Story,
Runcorn,
Cheshire,
England,
2020

Multiform offers endless
possibilities for reuse and
renewal. Studio MUTT's
proposed conversion of
a 1970s shopping-centre
car park into a series of
new social and cultural
community spaces shows
Multiform's potential
for both civic and
environmental renewal.

the selfie, clip-on cladding systems, Netflix, online food deliveries, auto-tune, Zoom meetings and the podcast. Multiform is a universal sensibility manifested in the particular, the one-off and the hybrid.

If Multiform is the conscious and unconscious response to a world in flux – economic, political and technological – the question arises of how and by what mechanisms that base connects to the architectural superstructure. What is the filling in that sandwich? This is the task put to the contributors to this ⅅ issue.

The issue begins by looking at the origins and motivations of Multiform's formal tactics. Lera Samovich explores the systematic improvisation of Porto-based fala atelier. Mario Carpo takes the long view, exploring 'chunkiness' from the Renaissance to Postmodernism. Studio MUTT and Office S&M each reflect on the formation of their own aesthetic eclecticism, while US architect and educator Jennifer Bonner explores the tactic of 'colour blocking'.

The importance of context – both urban and of media – is a recurring characteristic of Multiform. Stephen Parnell considers ⅅ's own role as a vehicle for postmodern ideas in the 1980s in relation to today's Instagram culture. Dirk Somers of Antwerp-based Bovenbouw argues for an accommodation between aesthetic order and anarchy in the urban landscape, while CAN's Mat Barnes celebrates the possibilities afforded by the city's ad-hoc formations, and Groupwork founder Amin Taha relates how exhaustive research – counterintuitively – allows for the unexpected. Léa-Catherine Szacka considers the domestic role of the screen in the 1980s and today. The artist and designer Camille Walala discusses the inspiration behind her colourful work, which has enjoyed notable success on the screen as well as in the city.

Then there are Multiform's inheritances. David Kohn explores architecture's ability to sustain multiple interpretations and identities, while DK-CM's David Knight and Cristina Monteiro assimilate the divergent legacies of the postwar and postmodern eras. Finally, AOC founder Geoff Shearcroft reflects on the absence of joy in architecture today, a call picked up in the inspiring work of designer Yinka Ilori.

It is naturally perverse to try to define a tendency which is characterised by its variety. But Multiform is not a style. There is no Multiform*ism*. Multiform is resistance to grand narratives, which will inherently take multiple forms. It exists in its non-conformity. Multiform is avowedly political without being 'for' any group or position. It believes in the profound importance of architecture to society. If Multiform is for anything, it is architecture for itself. ⅅ

Notes
1. Charles Jencks and Nathan Silver, *Adhocism: The Case for Improvisation*, Secker and Warburg (London), 1972.
2. Rory Olcayto, 'FAT: Back from the Dead to Edit The Architects' Journal', *Architects' Journal*, 4 August 2015: www.architectsjournal.co.uk/news/fat-back-from-the-dead-to-edit-the-architects-journal/8687119.article.
3. Robert Venturi, Denise Scott Brown and Steven Izenour, *Learning From Las Vegas: The Forgotten Symbolism of Architectural Form*, The MIT Press (Cambridge, MA), 1977, p 1.
4. Charles Jencks and Nathan Silver, *Adhocism: The Case for Improvisation*, Anchor Books (Garden City, NY), 1973, p 73. First published in 1972.
5. *Ibid*.
6. *Ibid*.

fala atelier,
House along a Wall,
Porto, Portugal,
2018

The main space is defined through
the geometry of a terrazzo floor
pattern and a number of carefully
placed elements. The flying
kitchen-counter, three green
doors and a circular opening
imply possible usages while also
suggesting a certain complexity.

Lera Samovich

Aiming **for** Personality

An Exercise of **Continuous Improvisation**

Lera Samovich describes the cooler appropriation of Postmodernism in the work of fala atelier, based in Porto, Portugal, of which she has been a member since 2014. While borrowing from and influenced by previous Postmodernisms, the practice's designs combine disparate formal tropes, materials and styles to create a less ironic, more sensible, less ornament-dependent and more serious architecture.

Fala atelier is a naive architecture practice based in Porto. The office is many things, and it has many sides – a Postmodernist side, a Deconstructivist side, an occasional Baroque side, a Mannerist one even. Then there are some unavoidable classicist moments: order, hierarchy and symmetry still count. We are able to lightly shift back and forth in between those. It is not a paradigm shift, but rather an extension of our compositional abilities. Those languages and strategies work again today, but for different reasons. Postmodernism in this case is not an opposition or denial of Modernism, but rather a joyful manipulation of the selected grammar and syntax.

The practice is, in a way, a sum of parts. First of all is the 'brain' – geeky, enthusiastic, full of exotic yet conflicting references. Then there is its context of Porto and Portugal, which is, as every context, both dull and exciting, difficult and specific in its own way. The clients are usually a bit torturous, the project briefs are repetitive, the municipalities are simply morbid. Too many pieces to put together. Therefore, every project turns into an intricate adventure of packing those ambitions, obsessions and references into a narrow plot, a two-level building with two facades and three bedrooms, following all the height limits, many rules and regulations. The result of such a game is usually a peculiar animal. Architecture happens at the intersection of our ambitions and limitations – cheerfully making the most of the things that do come our way.

There was no actual Postmodernism in Porto, but there are what we call 'ugly ducks', those beautifully banal and awkward buildings built between the 1960s and 1980s. Fala goes against the immense nostalgia and 'fetishisation' of history that dominates the Faculty of Architecture of the University of Porto (FAUP) and the 'Oporto school', which consistently supports the purist ideas of the Modern Movement. Here, the only acceptable architecture is that of Álvaro Siza and Eduardo Souto de Moura, for example their International Contemporary Sculpture Museum (MIEC) and Abade Pedrosa Municipal Museum (MMAP) project in Santo Tirso, completed in 2012. Fala has instead developed an attitude of questioning the accepted order of things, rejecting the expected minimalism maybe, the vague 'Portuguese-ness'.

In many ways we are completely ignorant of the context. However historical continuity is a concern. A long list of favourite architects, rooms, plans, facades and buildings is a common ground of the office, its basic language. We collect traces, fragments and elements from all over the world to reassemble back here, using whatever is at hand and recombining it to create something new in an attempt to be constantly updating our vocabulary. We understand each other through references, most of which are from the last 60 or 70 years. There is not much fascination for Palladio or even Louis Sullivan. There is always a Japanese gang: Kazuo Shinohara, early Toyo Ito, Kazunari Sakamoto and

fala atelier,
House in Paraíso,
Porto, Portugal,
2017

The unnecessarily proud and exuberant building has a double personality and unorthodox inside spaces.

Itsuko Hasegawa. There is Robert Venturi and Denise Scott Brown, and Peter Märkli. The occasional Mario Botta. Sometimes Konstantin Melnikov will appear, sometimes Lina Bo Bardi.

As a reaction to sad backgrounds composed of many banal buildings (and as a consequence of those wild, mainly Japanese, references from the 1970s), fala's work aims at a strong language, a personality. Every project is a place of formal experiment, trying to stand out among uneventful buildings. Our House in Paraíso in Porto (2017) is a good example of such a mismatch, an overly glorified facade amongst shabby backyards and annexes. Perhaps we protest too much, deliberately making life difficult for ourselves. And there is no fascination for technology or sustainability – just an aspiration for architecture whose main concern is form and space. Not politics, ecology or any kind of social agenda.

Assimilating Fragments and References
The result of this thick web of references is fala's recent (and very postmodern) preoccupation with the definition of architecture as a language. Our architecture can be described as divided and fragmented, with an emphasis on its elements. But not the Deconstructivist kind. Our buildings still stand on their feet. Their parts are separate elements of a structure that sums up the whole. They attract or repel one another like objects in space. They clash to generate uncanny linguistic mistakes and accidents. Systems and isolated elements are also a consequence of working on small-scale projects, which offer the chance to control it all. We want this language to be both a stable structure and to have lots of play, to be

fluid and ambiguous. Fala's work is moving towards a pluralistic language, an arrangement of multiple rhetorical manoeuvres, metaphors, tropes, turns and masks, as evident in our House along a Wall (Porto, 2018).

We are immensely interested in form and composition. Playful geometries happen as a reaction to defined perimeters. The complexity is almost forced upon a project, as in the abundant spaces in Uneven House (Porto, 2019). The excess and the extreme poverty of every building. A balanced combination of exhaustion and exuberance. And to quote the 'godfather of Postmodernism', Charles Jencks: 'Post-Modern architecture is obviously concerned with more than pluralism and complexity, although these two key words begin to locate its centre.'[1]

fala atelier,
Uneven House,
Porto, Portugal,
2019

The stubborn composition of doors and openings is adorned by a few grandiloquent details of marble and mirrors.

The various forms and elements of our projects use colour in a compositional way to distinguish between them, such as in House in Fontaínhas (Porto, 2019). When it comes to paint, we are decisive, but still afraid of purple and orange, and we certainly cannot handle clients asking for beige and brown. This has been a gradual appropriation; fala's early projects are mostly white, and even now there is always a white background. Splashes of colourful elements against a perfectly neutral base, as in Six Houses and a Garden (Porto, 2019) with some heart-warming wood and chilly marble, millennial pink and its ambivalent girliness.

There is an intense concern for patterns and ornaments. There is no architecture without decoration. Buildings are complex canvases and systems, or simple boxes with elaborate ornaments. The office quickly got bored with the minimalist surfaces of white plaster. And we like Daniel Buren, the French conceptual artist, and therefore stripes, dots and chequerboard patterns. Fala's patterns are still very shy in a way – too geometrically correct. Small and big boxes with pictures on them, as in House and Atelier (Porto, 2018). Facades become abundant masks and billboards.

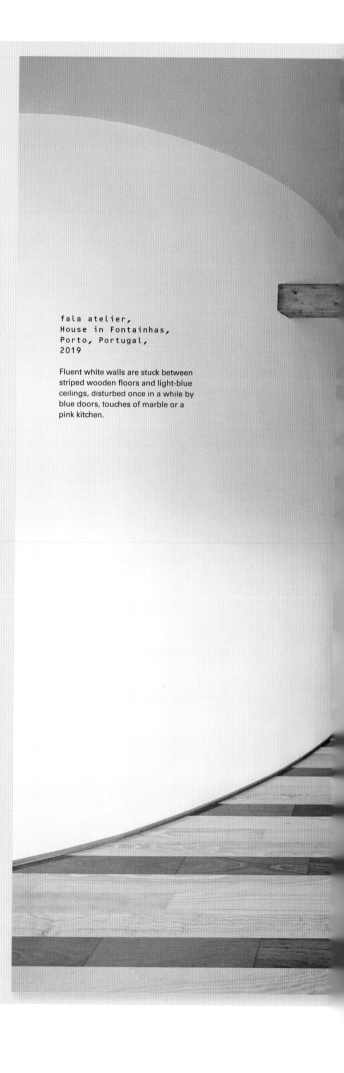

fala atelier,
House in Fontaínhas,
Porto, Portugal,
2019

Fluent white walls are stuck between striped wooden floors and light-blue ceilings, disturbed once in a while by blue doors, touches of marble or a pink kitchen.

fala atelier,
Six Houses and a Garden,
Porto, Portugal,
2019

The materiality of the awkward interiors follows their complexity. Walls are merely white, the horizontal slabs are abruptly concrete, the floors display polished blue marble, and the tilted ceiling is painted in pink. Wooden doors, exaggerated handles and hints of pink marble accompany the game of surfaces.

fala atelier,
House and Atelier,
Porto, Portugal,
2018

The soft chess-pattern is painted over a boxy hat that
is bluntly placed on top of the existing building.

Taking Things Seriously

Is fala postmodern? Yes, and no. Ultimately, ours is a circumstantial Postmodernism – a softer, more acceptable version of it. No neon signs, Doric columns or flower patterns. No swans on top of buildings. Postmodernism that is less ironic, less blunt and a bit more serious. Postmodernism that is based on grids, projections and orders. It does not go too far. It becomes one of the ingredients of a larger flamboyant cocktail. Any attempt at defining the language of the office does not yet seem precise or completely right. There is our deliberately systematic thinking on one side, and a slightly confusing linguistic behaviour on the other. To borrow another definition from Jencks: 'Architecture could again be based on context, mood, culture, ornament, or almost whatever mattered to the architect and client.'[2] The most sublime things result from precisely a confluence of opposites, a more playful and sophisticated use of unfriendly tropes. Fala's architecture is a continually renewed improvisation on themes coming from every possible direction. ᴈ

Notes
1. Charles Jencks, *The Language of Post-Modern Architecture*, Academy Editions (London), 1991, p 12. First published in 1977.
2. *Ibid*, p 10.

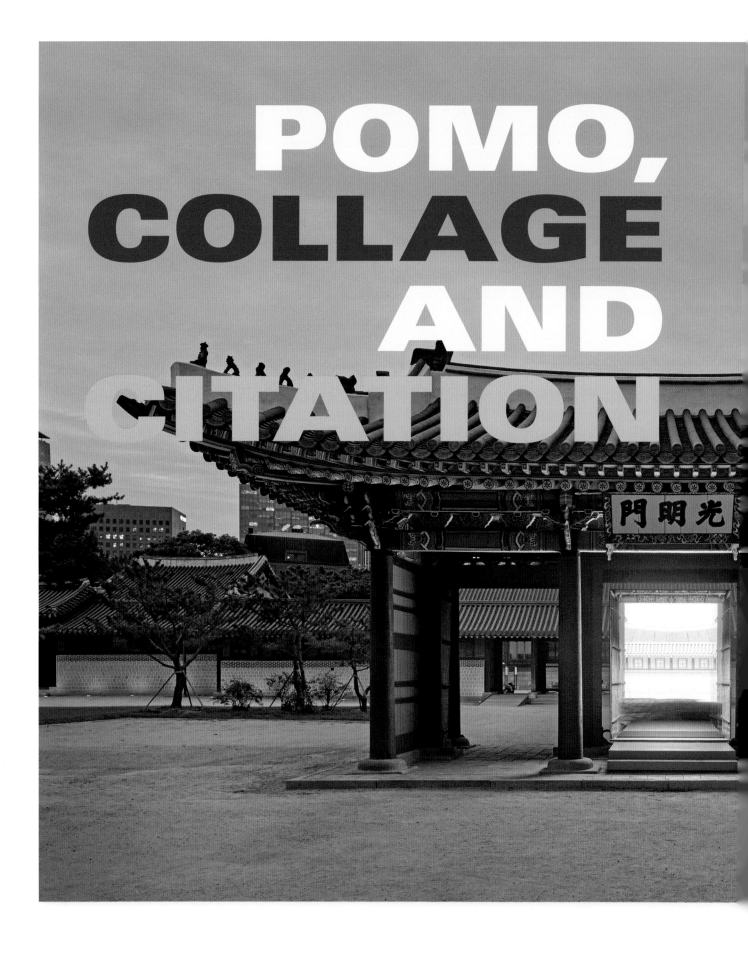

POMO,
COLLAGE
AND
CITATION

Mario Carpo

NOTES TOWARDS AN ETIOLOGY OF CHUNKINESS

Space Popular,
Gate of Bright Lights,
Seoul,
2019

London-based architects Space Popular created
a video installation positioned inside a doorway
of the historic Gwangmyeongmun Gate at
Deoksugung Palace in Seoul, Korea. The video
leads visitors through an exploration of traditional
dancheong-style gates before offering them the
glimpse of a new world.

There is an arc of 'chunkiness' (collage, montage and assemblage) which runs through much art and architecture, pulling together art practices and eras that at first seem very different from each other.

Mario Carpo, Reyner Banham Professor of Architectural Theory and History at the Bartlett, University College London and Professor of Architectural Theory at the University of Applied Arts in Vienna, eloquently takes us along its path.

Angelica Kauffmann,
Zeuxis Selecting Models for his Picture of Helen of Troy,
1794

The Greek painter Zeuxis (5th century BCE) famously composed the picture of one ideally beautiful woman by cutting and pasting details out of five real-life models. The epistemological and technical implication of his trans-mimetic design method never stopped puzzling classical artists.

We can make things by taking a chunk of solid matter, as found, then removing matter from it as needed, until we get to the shape we had in mind; or we can proceed the opposite way, by picking and choosing a number of smaller chunks, either found or made, and adding them to one another, somehow, until we get to a bigger chunk. When we make stuff the additive way the smaller chunks, parts or ingredients we mix and match may either show in the final product, or they may merge in a single, uniform block. In the latter case, we end up with a monolith – although an artificial, not a natural one in this instance. In the former case, we have a heteroclite (in the etymological, not in the current sense of the term): a whole that is made of discernible, discrete or separate parts.

In classical antiquity art was an imitation of nature. As nature often produces monoliths (example: a big boulder), while purposeful heteroclites are generally the result, hence the sign, of human laboriousness (example: a dry-stone wall), classical artists aimed at merging the parts of their composition in a single, uniform, smooth and homogeneous whole – as smooth as if made by nature itself. This principle is somewhat covertly implied in one of the most influential topoi (anecdotes, legends or parables) of classical art – one of those apparently dumb little stories that the Greeks and Romans often used in lieu of a fully fledged theory of what we now call the visual arts. This is the story, as told, among others, by Cicero and Pliny: the famed Zeuxis, the best-paid painter of his time, was invited to a town in what would now be southern Italy to paint a picture of a goddess. In search of inspiration he asked to see some examples of local beauties. The town elders sent him a selected group of handsome young men. Zeuxis protested, and he was then allowed to see some girls, but finding none quite to his taste, he retained five of them as models. His painting merged features taken from all five, and it met with great success – hence the lasting popularity of the anecdote. From the point of view of art theory however, and even of the theory of human knowledge, this seemingly innocent tale conceals a number of major theoretical conundrums, and the technicalities of Zeuxis's mode of artistic operation – the parsing, selection and reassembly of parts coming from many models – have invited a never-ending stream of theories and speculations. Evidently, the artist would not have limited himself in this instance to just cutting and pasting a number of pieces, as in a jigsaw puzzle; he would most likely have had to rework, modify and adapt some of the parts somehow, in order to make them fit in and blend with one another. Hence the question: how much of Zeuxis's operation was what we could call today a collage, and how much of it would have been some looser form of imitation – the work of a talented artist only vaguely and distantly inspired by some of his models, or sources? Could people look at his finished painting and tell: see, these are Emily's eyes, Peggy's nose and Nancy's lips? Or did he blend all of his sources in one transfigured, truly supernatural composition, where one would say: see, there is a certain something in this portrait that reminds me of Emily, and of Peggy, and of Nancy, but it's hard to tell what, precisely, comes from each? This is where, in classical theory, art would have equalled nature, because this is the way nature works: this is the way a father looks similar to his biological son.

The Modern Chunkiness of Mechanical Modularity

This 'organic' mode of composition, aiming at what we would now call design unity, and seen in classical antiquity and then again by many Renaissance Humanists as closer to nature's own processes, would be challenged by the early modern rise of the technical logic of mechanical making. Modern mechanical making typically uses casts, dies, moulds, stamps, or other kinds of mechanical matrixes to reproduce identical copies; as each matrix costs money, it makes sense to use it many times, to spread its costs over many copies; the more copies are made, the cheaper each copy will be. A typical design strategy to maximise economies of scale in a mechanical production workflow consists in using the same modular components in many different products, thus making more different products out of fewer, mass-produced identical parts. This is why the same headlamps or dashboards are used in many different models and makes of automobiles, for example. The iron logic of industrial modularity must have been evident from the earliest days of mechanical reproductions, but printed books, in particular – the earliest item of mechanical mass-production in the West – brought about a new perception of the modularity of artistic creation (hence a new appreciation of chunky art) due to a slightly more circuitous set of reasons.

Reviving classical Latin – Cicero's Latin in particular – had long been a core project of early modern Humanism. Around the time when Columbus discovered America a Renaissance Humanist, everywhere in Europe, was in the first instance a specialist in the imitation of Cicero – someone who could write in Latin as well as Cicero once did, and in the same style; to recall and reuse Cicero's words and expressions in their own writing Humanists often ended up learning Cicero's texts by heart. Then books, always rare and expensive, were suddenly made cheap and ubiquitous by the new technology of print, and scholars soon realised that they could easily keep the entire Ciceronian corpus on their desktops to consult at will. Printed indexes, thesauri and the alphabetical or thematic sorting of content made textual searches and information retrieval easier than ever before. As a result, citing and quoting, cutting and pasting (sometimes literally) from such easily available sources became pervasive and even fashionable; and with that, the notion that every new text could be composed as the semi-automatic assemblage of prefabricated (or, indeed, pre-written) textual fragments, or a mosaic (the technical term of the time was a cento) of ready-made citations. Early in the 16th century the elegant Humanist Erasmus even wrote a perfidious – and, at the time, hugely popular – pamphlet against the new fad of cut-and-paste composition. To no avail: citationist writing kept spreading, and soon some even started to theorise it. Prominent among these, the Neo-Platonist polymath Giulio Camillo (also known at the time for his talents as a lion tamer) built his mysterious Memory Theatre as a mechanical tool meant to facilitate the disassembly and recomposition of Cicero's writings. In Camillo's theory, every new text is a collage of older textual chunks – in that instance, each and all carefully and exclusively excerpted from the corpus of Cicero's original writings; but the principle was so widely applicable that it could be easily extended to other contexts and contents.

And it was. Camillo's interest in architectural theory is documented; he was also a friend of Sebastiano Serlio. As Camillo explained in a long-lost manuscript (found and published only in 1983) the analogy between the architect's job, and the writer's, is self-evident: Humanist writers, like him, wanted to use Cicero's language to express new ideas; Humanist architects, like Serlio, wanted to use the language of classical architecture to build new buildings; therefore, the programme being the same, architects and writers could use the same rules to play the same game. When translated into architectural terms, Camillo's cut-and-paste, or citationist method meant: establishing a corpus of chosen monuments of classical antiquity; breaking them up into smaller chunks, cut into sizes fit for combining with others in new compositions; last, compiling and publishing a catalogue of ready-made parts complete with the instructions needed for their assembly – as in an IKEA kit today. Strange as it may appear today, this is exactly what Serlio did, starting in 1537. His multi-volume, multi-instalment treatise in print, which was for long hugely influential, particularly in Northern Europe and in Protestant countries, did not contain actual spolia from old buildings, but it featured a long list of virtual modular chunks, duly sorted according to a sophisticated arborescent hierarchy, each drawn in plan, elevations and section, together with sets of rules for the redesign of each chunk at different scales and in different contexts if needed. These rules did allow for some leeway and occasional alterations in the design of each part, but a drawing (and a building) made by the montage of many chunks is bound to look chunky. Serlio unapologetically acknowledged that, proudly showing off – sometimes even emphasising – the whacky chunkiness of his designs as a way to call attention to the unusual spirit and very untimely ambition of his programme. For his was a deliberately mechanical design method, meant to teach the basics of good architecture to all and sundry; meant to turn design into a professional, socially responsible, run-of-the-mill technical operation. Not surprisingly, Serlio never had good press – and remains to this day unpopular among design scholars (whereas Michelangelo's coeval and at times even more obnoxious architectural chunkiness has often been more generously appraised). But through Serlio's work, and partly as a side effect of his notoriety as a philistine *avant la lettre*, architectural chunkiness earned an early and equally unpalatable, albeit at the start mostly subliminal reputation as the outward and visible sign of a mechanistic view of the world – the view of a modern world that was then barely dawning.

Such mechanical connotations became inescapable when, a few centuries later, Modernist art started to tackle, critique and question the technical logic of industrial mass-production. Braque's, Picasso's and Gris's collages were assemblages of printed (or stencilled) typographical characters, of mechanically printed wallpaper, or of actual newspaper pages; Duchamp's ready-mades were montages of standard items of mass-production: bicycle wheels, snow shovels, bottle racks. To make a long story short, throughout the 20th century assemblage, montage, collage, cut-and-paste and citation were primary attributes of the machine-made environment, as well as pertinently seen as such when used as artistic devices. Chunkiness in the arts stood for industrial modernity,

Title page of Sebastiano Serlio's *Third Book*, 1540

Architecture as fragmentation and recombination of ready-made parts (in this instance, ideal fragments from classical archetypes).

Sebastiano Serlio, gateway 29 from his *Extraordinary Book*, 1551

A deliberately ungainly assembly of obnoxious chunks, designed to please the 'bestial' taste of degenerate clients – here from a woodcut reprint in the Venice edition of 1584.

because industrial mass-production, assembly-line modularity and standardisation tend to generate chunky stuff. Each fabricated part can of course be as streamlined as needed, but the technical logic of mechanical assembly still requires that separate chunks, no matter how smooth, be joined together in a heteroclitic, hence chunky whole.

The Postmodern Chunkiness of Historicist Citation, Fragmentation and Intertextuality

Fast forward to the end of modernity – and to the postmodern turn of the late 1970s. Given the state of affairs I have just described, collage and citation should have been, back then, unlikely candidates for PoMo adoption. If you are a PoMo militant in, say, 1978, why would you care for a set of stylistic signifiers and compositional devices that were then universally seen as staples and icons of modernity – ie of your own chosen enemy? Yet, as we now know, PoMos of all ilk soon embraced citationist chunkiness without any reservations, and apparently oblivious to the Modernist lineage and credentials of mechanical collaging, gluing and pasting. This unexpected development was mostly due to one book and to the influence of one of its two authors. Colin Rowe had begun his career by claiming that, some four centuries apart, Palladio and Le Corbusier were in fact up to the same thing – one in plan, the other in elevation. One generation later, the anti-Modernist crusade of Colin Rowe scored another home run. The core argument of his *Collage City* (1978, with Fred Koetter) was that architects had been led astray by their faith in technology and science or, in other cases, by their subservience to popular taste. As an antidote to both fallacies Rowe suggests that architects should re-establish 'a sceptical distance from big visions of social deliverance',[1] ie architects should abandon all hope and ambition of doing something good for the rest of the world. As practical means to that end, Rowe offers two models: collision city, the city of bricolage, of which the archetype is Hadrian's Villa in Tivoli; and collage city, the city as a museum, of which Rowe's best example is Biedermeier or Restoration Munich (the historicist city of von Klenze and von Gärtner); Rowe's second choice was, oddly, the little town of Novara in Piedmont. Both collision city and collage city, as their names suggest, are assemblages of disjointed fragments – ie they are seen as the result of relatively uncoordinated additive processes, in the absence of a unified urban design; in the case of collage city, the fragments are citations – and in the case of Munich, verbatim replicas – of monuments from different periods of architectural history, mostly referring to the classical tradition (and it may as well be that British-born Rowe, 1920–1999, did not know any other).

So there you go: in a few pages, thanks to Rowe's droning and often vapid, wordy prose, Braque's and Picasso's Modernist collage was turned into a formal game of linguistic reference to the history of European classicism; and chunkiness and disjointedness, often the sign of the belligerent or antagonistic attitude of so many activist avant-gardes in the visual arts, became the *signe identitaire*, and the rallying cry, of a new wave of architects whose main project was to have none. To be noted, Rowe was not alone in plotting that chart back then, and in many ways his collage urbanism was very much in the spirit of the time: the itinerary of the architectural collage, from Modernist modularity to historicist

Giovanni Battista Piranesi,
Hadrian's Villa: remains of the Smaller Palace
(formerly called the Temple of Apollo),
from *Vedute di Roma,*
c 1768

In the 1970s Colin Rowe chose Hadrian's Villa in Tivoli and Biedermeier Munich as the archetypes of his anti-modern 'collage city' – a city made of heteroclitic, disjointed, chunky citations.

If you are a PoMo militant in, say, 1978, why would you care for a set of stylistic signifiers and compositional devices that were then universally seen as staples and icons of modernity - ie of your own chosen enemy?

John Outram,
Isle of Dogs
Pumping Station,
London, 1988

Collage, cut-and-paste and citations above and beyond Colin Rowe's rosier expectations. By the late 1980s, intertextuality – originally a powerful semantic device – came to be seen as a meaningless or jocular game of references.

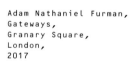

Adam Nathaniel Furman,
Gateways,
Granary Square,
London,
2017

Revival of the Chunk: for reasons
difficult to explain, and perhaps
inexplicable, chunkiness is
ubiquitous today – the visual
marque of socially conscious
computational brutalists (Gilles
Retsin, Daniel Kohler and Jose
Sanchez, among others), as
well as the battle cry of a new
generation of media-alert post-
digital designers, such as Adam
Nathaniel Furman, and of many
anti-tech, politically conservative
neo PoMos.

Charles Moore,
Piazza d'Italia,
New Orleans, Louisiana,
1978

opposite: Historical or historicist citations have always been bearers of meaning. A pledge of allegiance to the Western classical tradition (and to Roman Catholicism) in Louisiana may have been seen as a harmless architectural prank in 1978; it would be seen quite differently today.

The spectacular rise of postmodern design in the late 1970s – particularly in Europe – was primarily driven by the writings and ideas of Charles Jencks

THE LANGUAGE OF
POST-MODERN ARCHITECTURE
CHARLES JENCKS

ACADEMY EDITIONS

citation, is parallel and similar to the coeval drift of the critical notion of intertextuality, born as a technical offshoot of modern structural linguistics with Julia Kristeva and Roland Barthes in the late 1960s and early 1970s, but which would soon thereafter come to mean something akin to a theory of endless textual referentiality – a game of mirrors whereby, via citations or allusions, a text deliberately refers to another, and then to another, ad libitum and to the detriment of denotative meaning. So for example Jean-Luc Godard's references to the history of cinema and to film theory in his Nouvelle Vague masterpieces of the early 1960s were meant to hone cinema's power as a militant art of the index; Quentin Tarantino's game of citations in *Pulp Fiction*, to quote a famous line from the movie itself, 'doesn't mean a thing' (Butch's actual line to Esmeralda Villalobos in episode 5 of the movie cannot be quoted verbatim). *Pulp Fiction* has no message at all. It does not convey any urgent 'vision of social deliverance'. It is a postmodern movie.

For all Colin Rowe's formidable and lasting influence, most notably in American academia, the spectacular rise of postmodern design in the late 1970s – particularly in Europe – was primarily driven by the writings and ideas of Charles Jencks. Collage and citation, whether of the historicist kind or not, had no role in Jencks's theories of postmodernity. Sure, some of the buildings he championed, starting with his seminal *Language of Post-Modern Architecture* (1977),[2] looked conspicuously chunky, yet Jencks does not appear to have devoted any attention to chunkiness as a critical or stylistic category. For Jencks, unlike Rowe, did have a 'vision of social deliverance'. Jencks's mission was to liberate humankind from the shackles of industrial, mechanical mass-production. Jencks always saw architecture as a means, not as an end in itself; his Postmodernism always had a strong and very modern messianic component. This is why Jencks soon realised that the best way to advance his PoMo project was to spring forward, by means of technical change – not to fall backward, by dint of chunky fragments and historicist collage. But the part of the story that would follow from there is already well known. ⌀

Notes
1. Colin Rowe and Fred Koetter, *Collage City*, The MIT Press (Cambridge, MA), 1983, p.143 (first published 1978).
2. Charles Jencks, *The Language of Post-Modern Architecture*, Academy Editions (London), 1977.

Title page of Charles Jencks's
The Language of Post-Modern Architecture,
1977

The cover features the gaudy assembly of chunks in Minoru Takeyama's Ni-Ban-Kahn (Building Number Two, Tokyo, 1970).

Graham Burn,
James Crawford and
Alexander Turner

Studio MUTT,
Multi-Story,
Runcorn, Cheshire,
England,
2020

Multi-Story proposes turning the barrier-like car park of Runcorn Shopping Centre (1972) into an outward-facing entrance point for pedestrians, while reintroducing to the retail-heavy 'town centre' a mix of much-needed social functions: markets, food and drink, sports pitches, music practice rooms, craft rooms, table tennis and climbing walls.

HING

REFERENCING,
REMIXING
AND SAMPLING

Liverpool and London practice Studio MUTT's Graham Burn, James Crawford and Alexander Turner **contend** that **the current age of** unpredictable transition is **not the** time for pseudo-radical **newness. Instead,** they evoke **the concept of** the 'sample' **as their mode** of creative architectural practice, **propounding** it **as an** appropriate modus **operandi for the** contemporary political, pandemic **and dwindling** neo-liberal **condition.**

A remix is a piece of media, most commonly music, which has been altered from its original state by adding, subtracting or changing it in some way to create something new. Remixing as we think of it today has its roots in 1970s Jamaican dancehall culture, which was then taken to New York where disco producers gave us the live-action collage of cutting and scratching in early hip hop. Through editing, layering and combining with other source material, a hook or lick can be turned into something that is at once familiar and peculiar.

For Studio MUTT, this is why sampling and remixing is such a potent tool in architecture. As a process it resists the urge for superficial 'newness', but, due to the complex negotiations of site, client and technology, nonetheless creates something that is particular and fresh.

At the heart of the tactic of using references, samples and remixing is the connection people have to that which is familiar, and how meaning can be transferred, carried and combined with other artefacts to form something new, but with embedded meaning. It opens doors to various ways of communicating through design.

POSTMODERN ROOTS

Many early Postmodernists sought to re-engage architecture's communicative potential through linguistics, deploying various arguments around a language of design. However, language is only a small part of how we communicate. It is why video calling is so exhausting – it is difficult to read the room via webcam, so we have to work without our usual social intuitions and rely on language alone.

As a way of widening the field of architectural communication beyond simple linguistic analogies, a number of postmodern architects looked to referencing and sampling as a way of communicating in architecture. Although varied, the approach is mostly typified by an in-your-face Pop art style. The unapologetic reappropriation of signs and symbols lent legitimacy to new types of business on one hand, and attempted to reconnect with history on the other.

Ian Pollard,
Sainsbury's Homebase,
Kensington, London,
1988

Pollard's provocative questioning of authorship, authenticity and originality, with wit and humour were all exciting lines of enquiry. But it was by no means the most considered or crafted building – the latter common criticism of postmodern buildings – and it was sadly demolished in 2014.

An important example for Studio MUTT was Ian Pollard's neo-Egyptian Homebase store in Kensington, London (1988), a spectacularly strange place that we often visited for studio supplies as students. Structurally it was a big metal shed, as you would expect for a large retail unit. But externally it was wrapped in a mysterious facade incorporating a ruinous Egyptian colonnade, an engraved mural complete with a power-tool-wielding Egyptian god, striped stone-cladding and a miniature replica of the lime-green, double-curved window, cut and pasted from James Stirling and Michael Wilford's Neue Staatsgalerie in Stuttgart that was completed four years prior.

Like most pieces of Postmodern architecture from that period, Pollard's Homebase stirred conflicting emotions. For us the building was one tangible example of the intriguing eccentricity found in the postmodern period when architects scoured all eras, combining representational elements to produce work that was rich with memory and associative meaning. This could cause strange, often contradictory collages of information that were exhilarating, liberating and sometimes bizarre. Distant worlds were imported to create fictional narratives of place, borrowing and stealing from other sources to create new, complex arrangements of ideas that went beyond the singular object.

All of this played out during the late 1970s and 1980s against the backdrop of the dawn of neoliberalism, which prompted a period of profound change in society and culture. The question is, what relevance do these postmodern strategies have today at a time of similar transition?

NEWNESS

Climate change, a potential age of pandemics and economic uncertainties have revealed the frailty of neoliberalism and its struggle to cope with such challenges. Its successor is still unknown but, just as in the 1980s when neoliberalism took the reins from Keynesianism as the dominant economic system, there will undoubtedly be significant shifts in all our lives.

It is tempting to answer the current calls for 'change', 'new normals' and 'new beginnings' with architecture that strives to be new and sweeps away the past to bring about a 'new utopia'. But we have been here before. Modernism answered equivalent calls in the 1920s and 1930s, and then again in the postwar era. And while it did much necessary and admirable work, for some, Modernist newness became a fetish, prioritised over everything else, striving for unprecedented forms and genius-like originality, siteless and unrelated to past architectures.

This quest for 'newness' still permeates architectural culture today. It still leads to 'new' architecture that rejects the real-world condition it finds itself in and quickly becomes irrelevant, or requires significant resources to be refurbished, rebuilt, relaunched and rebadged to the point of absurdity.
It is an architectural equivalent of Sisyphus, meaninglessly pushing the boulder up the mountain.

Studio MUTT,
The Lawyer, In Character,
'Out of Character',
Sir John Soane's Museum, London,
2018

above: The starting point for the 'Out of Character' exhibition was Soane's 1812 manuscript 'Crude Hints Towards an History of My House', in which he imagines his home as a ruin, stumbled upon by future ancestors who speculate on its use, occupants and origins. *The Lawyer* referenced and sampled material from the museum to create a stacked assemblage looking out over Lincoln's Inn Fields – home to the Inns of Court of the same name.

Studio MUTT,
The Architect, In Character, 'Out of Character',
Sir John Soane's Museum, London,
2018

right: The Architect was installed amongst Soane's collection of casts and architectural fragments of buildings that he saw on his Grand Tour to Rome and Naples, via Paris, in 1778–80. Its forms reference Soane's fascination with Egyptian architecture, which he would have seen as one of the precursors of classical architecture.

Studio MUTT,
James Street Hotel,
Liverpool,
2020

The hotel sits within the city's UNESCO World Heritage Site.
In response to the historic context, the elevation synthesises
the grand, heavy masonry architecture of the area into a
chequerboard of rusticated stone textures and deep setbacks.

Referencing, remixing and sampling are themselves nothing new and go back to the very beginnings of our architectural culture. Yet part of the lure for us is the outrage they still provoke among the more pious sections of the profession who see these processes as unethical and a contradiction of their still-Modernist principles of honesty and originality.

The use of reference as a design tool was instilled into the studio early on by our inspirational tutor David Dunster, who made it clear that copying was far from criminality. 'Everyone copies' and 'copy someone else and do it better' were a couple of his favourite phrases, along with 'never trust a man wearing grey shoes', which to this day is slightly harder to understand. The leap from using copying and improving as a creative act to referencing was a natural one.

The sample in architecture is as much a part of Studio MUTT's process as it is a symbolic or expressive product. It can reveal itself in form or detail, material or spatial sequence, and be figurative or abstract. Importantly, samples are often based on moments, whether studied or from memory, which are then remixed with the rich world of references that orbit around a specific project. This was particularly the case in 'Out of Character', an exhibition at Sir John Soane's Museum, London, in 2018. Here we installed four interventions that were either very small buildings or very large models that remixed references to create the four characters described by Soane in 'Crude Hints Towards an History of My House' (1812),[1] a strange text in which he imagines his house as a ruin and speculates on who visitors might think had lived there.

Our ongoing project for a hotel on James Street, Liverpool, the prominent waterfront site with illustrious neighbours in

Norman Shaw and Herbert Rowse, called for a different approach. Here the idea was to synthesise the bold, heavyweight and rugged masonry architecture of the grand surroundings in the elevation, through deep setbacks and a chequerboard of rusticated stone textures.

There is a depth and richness to architectural culture. In the film *Satchmo the Great* (1957),[2] legendary jazz musician Louis Armstrong reduces music to two types: good or bad. The same goes for architecture. The age, style or type of reference is largely unimportant, but is simply broken down into the same two categories, good or bad. Studio MUTT tries to use the good type, as seen in the context of each specific project.

Studio MUTT's work stands against the vacuous and reactionary architecture of late-neoliberalism and the pseudo-radicalism of the pursuit of the new. The studio's approach instead draws from our vast common architectural lineage, while also interrogating its own set of specific conditions, as illustrated in our recent project – Multi-Story – that reimagines a multilevel car park in Runcorn, Cheshire, as the focal point of the town's sociocultural life.

It is unclear what lies beyond neoliberalism, but if architecture is to remain socially relevant then it must engage in the everyday world and our shared cultural experience. Referencing, remixing and sampling allow architecture to negotiate between continuity and change, which is vital in such shaky times. ⌂

Notes
1. Sir John Soane, *Crude Hints Towards an History of My House in Lincoln's Inn Fields*, Archaeopress Publishing (London), 2015.
2. *Satchmo the Great*, 1957. Director Edward R Murrow, CBS, US.

The hotel site lies on the edge of the gridded urban layout of the historical district. This view from the 'Three Graces' – Liverpool waterfront's neoclassical showpiece – reveals how the building's strong corner redefines the edge of the urban block.

Jennifer Bonner

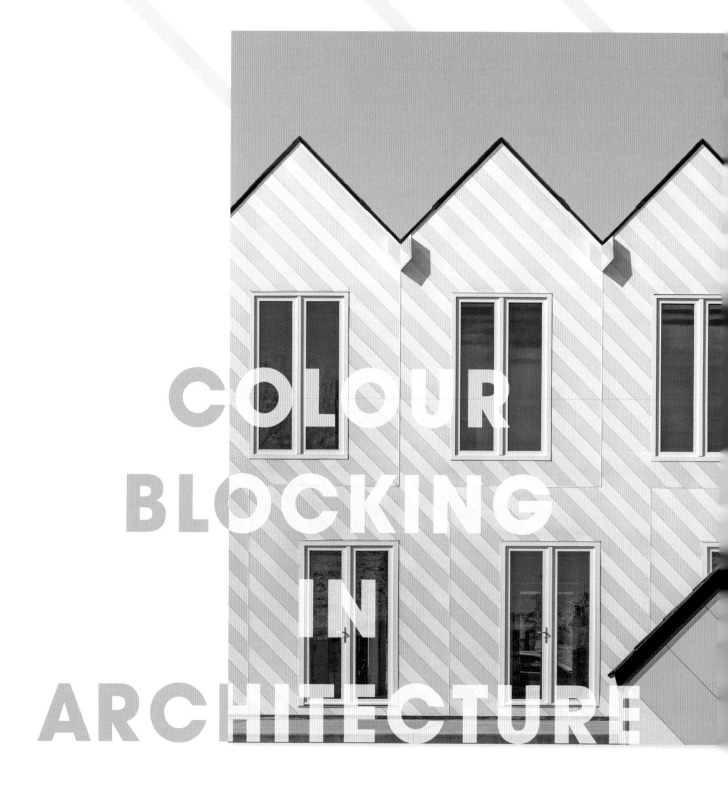

COLOUR
BLOCKING
IN
ARCHITECTURE

A repetitive exterior material block is stamped out in
yellow stripes to cover a four-bay elevation.

MARNI
SWEATERS
AND
RUGBY
SHIRTS

Architects are making colour fashionable again. This started slowly, but now the change is accelerating within the architectural profession. Jennifer Bonner, Associate Professor of Architecture at the Harvard University Graduate School of Design (GSD) and Founding Principal of MALL, illustrates this assertion with a collection of colourful examples and assesses their similarities and differences.

Architects used to wear all black, now they wear colour. It was slow at first; male colleagues wore colourful socks and if you did not glance down at the ground you might miss those bright ankles peeking out of their pant legs. One architect was photographed wearing a navy button-down shirt with a canary-yellow bow tie. I only saw his portrait once, but I remember that colour palette and that look. Delicate floral shirt, gingham tie, and paisley pants would be what might be called 'material block' – three misfit patterns, all at once. All or nothing.

On another instance, an architect was wearing camel-brown pants (or was it a caramel colour?) and matching Air Force 1s. The colours were a perfect match – how did they do it? I once tried to convince an architect to buy a tan shirt that looked like a paper bag. It was crinkly and reminded me of their architecture. It would have paired well with a soft pink, also in their repertoire.

Then, almost by brute force, the chunky blocks of colour walked into the room. They were women with turquoise tights, yellow tops and mint-green trousers. They wore colourful Converse and magenta geometric necklaces with thickly striped blouses. In architectural photographs of their buildings they stood in as scale figures and wore electric blue from head to toe and bubblegum-pink dresses. No one knew quite what to say except, 'oh, that's a lot of colour'. Once their budgets grew, it was less H&M and more COS, but the ultimate was the colour-block Marni sweater.

The widespread notion that architecture and colour – including what architects wear – have had a long precarious relationship with one another is misguided; architects have been working with – if not wearing – colour all along. It is precisely the way in which architects 'colour', and its generational tendencies, that require a closer look.

PRE-TEEN UNIFORMS: RUGBY SHIRTS OF THE 1980S
For purposes of furthering a definition, the work of six architects – Independent Architecture, MALL, FPEnterprise, Adam Nathaniel Furman, Project Room and MAIO – is used here to bring the role of aesthetics in contemporary culture, namely ways of colour blocking, into focus. In these architects' work the technique of colour blocking appears closely aligned with visuals found in contemporary culture outside the discipline, specifically located in fashion. 'In fashion' is something avant-garde architects staunchly resist, but 'in conversation with fashion' seems to be fair game.

Let us imagine this group of architects as pre-teens in the late 1980s sporting striped rugby shirts, with alternating chunks of colour. This fictional uniform is important and central to the argument. Overwhelmingly on-trend in popular culture at the time, forest-green and mustard-yellow stripes or sky-blue and Coca-Cola-red colour-block collared shirts were worn during the architects' formative years. These architectural pre-teens were dressing the part. And visual influence runs deep.

STRIPES
Independent Architecture's Motherhouse in Denver (2019), the stripes of which run proud on the exterior of this four-gabled single-family house, is a project that most closely aligns with the rugby shirt analogy. Canary yellow combined with what looks like lemon chiffon in alternating stripes is repetitive and underscores the strong image of its rhythmic roofline. The siding material hung parallel to one of the roof pitches is abruptly cropped before the next bay repeats again. The architects have their own conceptual reasons for misalignment, with nods towards historical precedents, but for the purposes of understanding what colour blocking might do in architecture, there is an alternate reading.

To conceive of each bay as a block of material, much like a stamp, colour in combination with pattern produces jarring repetition. Stripes are meant to cover an architectural form uniformly, but Independent Architecture's misaligned stripes applied in five sections across the length of a four-bay system inscribe bold colour on a normative rainscreen siding, serving to exaggerate what might otherwise be viewed as just a flat elevation. This colour-block technique is broken the moment it leaves the main house and travels to the accessory dwelling unit in the backyard where it reappears as a thicker colour block with a three-board pattern. Stripes shift and then swell in both house forms, suggesting a convincing alibi for elevational flatness.

BLOCKS

Less rugby shirt, more Marni sweater, MALL's Haus Gables in Atlanta (2018) uses colour blocking on the domestic interior at the scale of three rooms: a kitchen in black terrazzo tile, a bumblebee-yellow vinyl dining room and a master bedroom masked in a greyish marble-like vinyl together flatten the 17-metre (55-foot) long view from front to back of the house. Deploying both colour and material as blocks, the interior is covered with faux finishes on multiple surfaces. The floor and wainscoting are coordinated to produce visual continuity at the scale of an entire floorplate despite the jolting graphic break from one room to another. Blocks of colour intentionally offset the materiality of the cross-laminated-timber superstructure – and its Swedish spa association. Colour blocking creates a series of situational chromatic backdrops or programmatic sets to play out the mundanities of everyday life like washing dishes.

More compositional than a legible stripe, a Marni colour-block sweater suggests a mix of larger blocks of colour with lesser amounts applied to sweater cuffs or sleeves. This compositional imbalance is found in the work of Francesca Perani of FPEnterprise as she tackles hefty material blocks in her Urban Cabin (2019), a renovation in Bergamo, Italy. The apartment is fitted out with 90 per cent oriented strand board (OSB) and 10 per cent high-gloss Persian-indigo resin. But rather than mixing them, FPEnterprise dials up the sizable OSB block to encompass a one-room studio apartment as ceiling, wall, floor, cabinetry, door and built-in bench are all covered with one monotone material. The electric-blue punch, or pop, in contrast, is small by comparison, but refocuses attention on an unlikely space – the bathroom (or cuff) – shiny, glossy and cavernous.

CHUNKS

If FPEnterprise favours more of one and less of another to achieve material blocking, Adam Nathaniel Furman's Nagatachō Apartment in Tokyo (2019) evens out materials by overdoing it. Furman amplifies material and colour with equal parts of dazzlingly cheerful doorways and dizzyingly bright corridors. In-between spaces never looked so vivid. A range of colours are distributed as chunks: millennial pink, baby blue, lilac, neon green and orange turn corners, cross thresholds and break tradition within a small apartment interior. In any given architectural photograph, one can count a parade of six to nine colours on display. The colour-block takeaway: exaggeration of many colours in equal proportions smooth out and unify discrete domestic spaces.

Project Room, a trio of designers in Los Angeles, work through a whole spectrum of colours in the Farrow & Ball Showroom on La Cienega Boulevard in Los Angeles (2018). Arguing that the 'anonymity of the paint chip is replaced with a three-dimensional object',[1] the colour-blocking lesson here might be how Project Room applies colour to a series of objects, rather than walls or surfaces, to enhance architectural space. Their display is didactic, painting each object one by

Jennifer Bonner / MALL,
Haus Gables,
Atlanta, Georgia,
2018

above and below: A 17-metre (55-foot) long view through three domestic spaces covered in faux finishes creates a graphic colour block at the scale of a single floorplate.

Francesca Perani / FPEnterprise,
Urban Cabin,
Bergamo, Italy,
2019

The interior of this micro-apartment is a compositional
material block of 90 per cent oriented strand board
(OSB) and 10 per cent Persian-indigo resin.

Adam Nathaniel Furman,
Nagatachō Apartment,
Tokyo, 2019

Five colours distributed into assorted chunks
reimagine a domestic corridor.

MAIO,
110 Rooms,
22 Dwellings Housing Block,
Barcelona,
2016

Stairwells and elevator shafts are distinguished
by material and colour blocks to create a sectional
ground-floor plane.

Colourful totems on display at the Farrow & Ball Showroom illustrate how colour blocking in architecture is more three-dimensional and less of a surface treatment with endless possibilities for stacking.

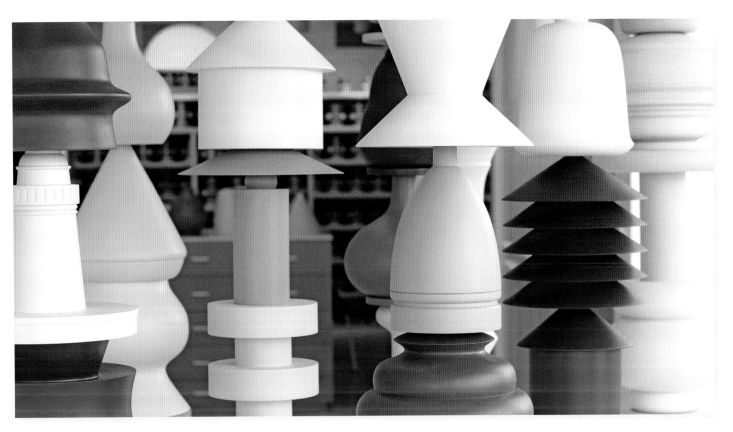

one for the consumer to sort through endless combinations of colour schemes. Doing so points towards another useful operation as colour blocking is applied to a set of discrete volumes that are colour coded, numbered and stacked up like totems. Grids or matrixes of colour are a way of the past in contrast to these abstract figures and geometric primitives – literal 'blocks' – using rotational forms to spin light around a room.

And finally, MAIO's 22 Dwellings Housing Block in Barcelona (2016) overstates architectural volumes by colour blocking stairwells and elevator shafts in combination with a sectional entry sequence. Similar to Project Room's totems, MAIO assigns material and colour to architectural objects clad in ochre, black, pink, emerald-green marble and light-grey stone to further complicate a ground-floor plan. Colour blocking on a straightforward, rectilinear plan does not work; MAIO's ground-floor plan is dynamic and so are its chunky materials and colours.

SHAKING THINGS UP

As architects' fashion sense shifts from head-to-toe default black clothing to wardrobes full of vivid colour combinations, connecting these visual tendencies with the analogy of a 1980s rugby shirt and Marni sweater offers another way to understand contemporary architecture. This argument is less about trends and more closely aligned with cultural aesthetics and observations about what we wear. Colour blocking is daring, graphic, and flattens

architectural space or, when used in reverse, has the capacity to turn a flat elevation into a volumetric mass. Blocks of materials are being specified by architects at the scale of the house or urban block, work best on dynamic floor plans, and challenge traditional corridors, entry and room arrangements. Overstated colour combinations, material exaggeration and the ways in which these architects 'colour' architectural space shake up subtle, mute and monotone architecture of recent years. Glaringly compositional, I can't help but see shirts and sweaters in contemporary architecture. Abstraction is out and composition is back. ᗄ

NOTE
1. www.projectroom.la/farrow-ball-showroom.

Text © 2021 John Wiley & Sons Ltd. Images: pp 32–3 © Independent Architecture, photo James Florio; p 35 © Jennifer Bonner, photos NAARO; p 36(l) © Francesa Perani, FPEnterprise; pp 36-7 © Jan Vranovský; p 38 © José Hevia; p 39 Courtesy of Project Room

MORE WITH LESS

Catrina Stewart and Hugh McEwen

RESPONDING TO AUSTERITY

Office S&M,
Mo-tel House,
Islington, London,
2020

Studies of characters and composition
of furniture pieces in the space.

London's Office S&M, formed by **Catrina Stewart and Hugh McEwen** just after the 2008 financial crash, has been honed in a decade of austerity. The practice has garnered a reputation for the innovative use of materials and a formal dexterity. By giving each project a narrative, they are able to deliver more with less.

Austerity has engendered a society that is risk averse, where background architecture is the norm and 'brick chic' is lauded. This has led planning authorities, politicians and royals to use contextualism as a tool for enforcing conformity and a singular way of designing. At one end of the spectrum, this endorses the New London Vernacular, where buildings must mimic the old – always the polite type of old – and at the other it results in full-on Trad. But the wheel of taste is turning, in the same way that Postmodernism emerged out of the deep recession of the late 1970s.

Established in the years following the 2008 crash, Office S&M has developed its work through 10 years of austerity in the UK. The practice's approach is a material response to the social, cultural and political conditions of today. Through a pluralistic architecture, Office S&M embraces Pop culture, emerging trends and technological advances to produce architecture as an experience. The office's built projects are a polemic tool to question the prevalent culture of architectural design, and illustrate the practice's approach to sustainability, material and economy in framing a response to austerity.

Built to Last

Through materials such as melted plastic, extruded aluminium and Blitzcrete, the practice looks at longevity rather than assuming material will always be available. Each project is investigated in terms of resources and social sustainability, as well as environmental sustainability. Considering lifespan, cost and lifecycle means that alternative approaches to the falsely assumed sustainability of traditional materials such as brick can be proposed.

Janus House (2018) was designed to replace a poorly built lean-to at the back of a Victorian terraced house in Walthamstow, East London. The budget was constrained, and through research into economical materials, Office S&M proposed a spray-on Prokol polyurea – originally developed to protect oil rigs – because of its low cost, seamless finish and contrast with the existing brickwork. The material is incredibly durable. It is sprayed on hot and cools instantly to form a thin yet protective layer over the structure. It is waterproof, does not weather, and has a guarantee for 60 years.

Invariably working with small budgets and sites has pushed the practice to make the most of these limits, but in contrast to many other approaches, Office S&M delivers a bounty of architecture, rather than being meagre with its designs.

Reuse, Reframe and Repurpose

Constraints are opportunities, and narrative provides an investigative route that can elevate the most prosaic of materials. The practice views waste material as being inherently valuable in its current state, rather than being interested in recycling it into a virgin form. Mo-tel House (2020) is a remodelling of a Georgian townhouse in Islington, London, for a client who founded Onloan, an online service that believes in lending fashion rather than consuming it. These ideas of borrowing and reuse were carried through in the materials and shapes of the project. Office S&M reused materials that had a story, such as surfaces made from melted milk bottles and terrazzo made from pulverised rubble, to form luxurious marbled worktops. Every material has been borrowed, reused and reframed for a new purpose. Synonymously, each piece

Office S&M,
Janus House,
Walthamstow, London,
2018

opposite top: The 'two-faced' rubber-coated rear elevation of the house. The side with the circular opening contains the bathroom, while the rectangular side is the kitchen.

opposite bottom: Prokol polyurea was sprayed onto a smooth plywood shell to form a seamless, watertight coating.

Through materials such as melted plastic, extruded aluminium and Blitzcrete, the practice looks at longevity rather than assuming material will always be available

The stair is designed as the entrance to
the space, and made from a layering of
narratives, colours and geometry.

Designing using narrative as much as material responds to a culture where people seek experiences over possessions

of furniture is designed to have more than one function, for example a bench that provides seating for the dining table also provides storage, a throne to play on, and a cabinet to display curiosities. These multiple functions allow each family member to find new uses for the furniture, and through this reinterpretation the object's own lifespan is extended. Designing using narrative as much as material responds to a culture where people seek experiences over possessions, and in this case the cohabitees wear shared haute couture rather than seeing the world as something to be infinitely consumed.

A Study in Generosity

By engaging with the current political landscape, Office S&M responds to contemporary ways of living. Salmen House (2017) is a new build-to-rent addition to a terrace in East London, designed as a study in generosity, rather than austerity, for its tenants and for the street it sits on. With more people renting privately, it offers flexibility for different tenants, with a bathroom for each bedroom, so that it can accommodate young professionals on a room-by-room basis, a nuclear family or an intergenerational family – the fastest-growing family unit in the UK.

Internally, generosity is expressed through a durable specification, double-height spaces and dual-aspect windows in each room. But these benefits have not come at a price, as the house was constructed for £205,000 meaning that the tenants pay standard market rates for a significantly better quality of housing. It is also well insulated, costing the tenants only £300 a year for heat, light and power.

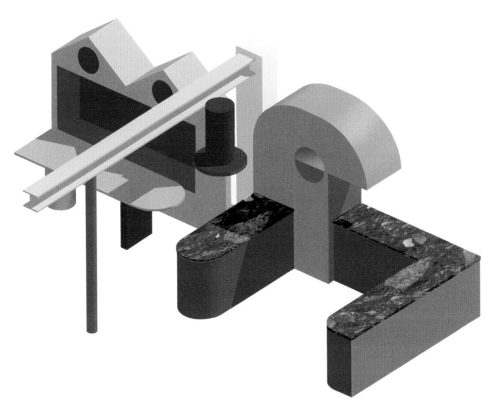

Office S&M,
Mo-tel House,
Islington, London,
2020

The fitted furniture pieces are imagined as characters in a story, intended for multiple uses, and existing at multiple scales.

Office S&M,
Salmen House, Plaistow,
London, 2017

The corner site is where two terraces meet.
The vertical windows, framed in polished
terrazzo, mirror the Victorian windows on the
right side, while the horizontal recesses are a
continuation of the mid-century terrace on the
left. The cranked and stepped front entrance
welcomes tenants into their house.

By clearly opposing
the New London
Vernacular, the
house is instead
an improvement
on its context,
rather than a copy

Though rented, the house is designed as a unique home. This is achieved by using colour, rich materials and detailing that responds to the best parts of its neighbours. The millennial-pink exterior breaks away from the traditional biscuit colour of rented accommodation. Colour is cheap, but stippled render and textured terrazzo have a material richness to them, catching changing shadows on the long flank wall throughout the afternoon. The house is generous to the street, giving something back rather than being overly polite to its context. By clearly opposing the New London Vernacular, the house is instead an improvement on its context, rather than a copy.

Reappropriation, Juxtaposition and Assemblage

Office S&M proposes a characterful, joyful and colourful alternative to 'austerity chic'. Each project is explored through reappropriation, juxtaposition and assemblage of elements. While the work is born out of austerity, through its economy of means it challenges the typical risk-averse, polite response of 'beige-itecture'. The office sees reuse as an essential design tool in a world where resources are finite: this is not a sacrifice, it is a luxury – more with less. ⌀

While the work is born out of austerity, it challenges the typical risk-averse, polite response of 'beige-itecture'

Office S&M,
Putnoe House,
Bedford, England,
2019

The house is designed from a family of 3D forms, wrapped together by a palette of cladding materials – grey shiplap weatherboarding, olive corrugated concrete and heather-glazed terracotta.

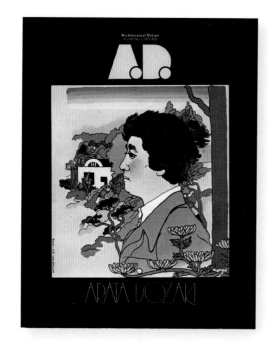

THE

AD Profile: *Arata Isozaki,*
January 1977

The first of the **AD** Profiles, which was a turning
point for the journal, not only in the quality of
production, but also the emphasis of style and
formalism. This was the first **AD** in which Charles
Jencks outlined his theories of Radical Eclecticism.

REBIRTH

OF A

MOVE

BIRTH AND

Stephen Parnell

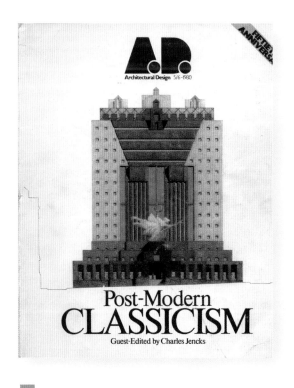

 Post-Modern Classicism,
May/June 1980

A new phase of Postmodernism emerged with the Venice
Architecture Biennale in 1980. This 'high' phase focused
on reinterpreting classical motifs for current architecture
and is arguably the one most commonly associated
with postmodern architecture. The cover shows Michael
Graves's design for the Portland Building in Portland,
Oregon, a straightforward office block adorned with
oversized classical motifs on the surface.

Charles Jencks's Postmodern Odyssey in AD

MENT

Architect and architectural historian **Stephen Parnell**, from Newcastle University's School of Architecture, Planning and Landscape, charts the evolution of Postmodernism in architecture, the critical role of Charles Jencks in theorising and propagating it and the seminal place ⚏ has in that history as the main publication that enabled its assimilation around the world.

⚏ Post-Modernism,
April 1977

Published to coincide with the launch of Jencks's *The Language of Post-Modern Architecture*, this issue marked the beginning of a campaign by Jencks and ⚏ to fight for pluralism in architecture.

One need only take a look at the issues of *Domus* from the period to realise that ⚏ was not the only magazine to promote Postmodernism in the 1980s. But with the well-connected Anglo-American historian and critic Charles Jencks using it as a vehicle to launch his ideas and fight for pluralism, ⚏ became almost synonymous with the movement as he and Andreas Papadakis's Academy Editions tirelessly promoted it as a style, an approach, or what Reinhold Martin has called a 'discursive formation'.[1]

THE RISE OF POSTMODERN ARCHITECTURE

Jencks held an unequivocal and definitive position: Modernism was dead and its replacement, Postmodernism, was to take its place. Jencks had been mulling over this idea since the early 1970s and tested it in a talk at Eindhoven in April 1975, which was later published in an article entitled 'The Rise of Post-Modern Architecture'.[2] His other strand of thinking, popular in architectural theory at the time, was semiotics, which formed the basis of his first book.[3] These two ideas merged into *The Language of Post-Modern Architecture* (first published in 1977),[4] which went on to sell over 160,000 copies over seven editions in 10 languages, and marked the beginning of the Papadakis/Jencks publishing phenomenon. Over the next 15 years, as Academy published six editions of this bestseller, four distinct phases of development of Postmodernism can be identified through the pages of ⚏, the magazine around which this successful collaboration orbited. The characteristics of these essentially define the many faces of Postmodernism with which we can compare any resurgence in interest in the movement today.

RADICAL ECLECTICISM

The first phase, which might be called 'Radical Eclecticism' after one of Jencks's early postmodern classifications, began with the publication of the first ⚏ Profile in January 1977. This new format was a turning point in ⚏'s history: not only was it a higher-quality production, but it was the first to promote style and formalism over the previous, more socially and politically conscious editorial line. It featured the work of Arata Isozaki, whose eclectic nature Jencks was already labelling in opposition to 'the tyranny of centralised culture',[5] or Modernist purism. He went on to claim that unless a theory for this Radical Eclecticism was developed, it too would fail, like its 19th-century weak eclectic counterpart, which he partially blamed for the emergence of the Modern movement. Jencks briefly outlined a version of this theory, describing Radical Eclecticism as a meaningful language that was able to communicate to both architects and the public.[6]

April 1977 saw the ⚏ *Post-Modernism* issue published to coincide with the launch of *The Language of Post-Modern Architecture*, and corresponding exhibition and symposium at Peter Cook's Art Net gallery in London.

This effectively signalled the arrival of postmodern architecture in the Anglo-Saxon world, with favourable articles, reviews and expositions on Jencks's book in the press. As the introduction to the ⚏ issue auspiciously stated: 'Several leading architects and architectural critics are of the opinion that the modern movement is at an end and that it is now being superseded by new work which they have taken to calling "post-modern".'[7]

Within a year, Jencks had already revised his book and the full new final chapter formed the basis of the January 1978 *Ɒ* *Post-Modern History* issue, which included Peter Eisenman, Robert Stern, Charles Moore, Venturi & Rauch and Michael Graves. *Ɒ*'s Radical Eclecticism phase lasted another three years and was characterised by a range of mostly historically orientated Profiles. The third edition of *The Language of Post-Modern Architecture*, revised and enlarged with a chapter called 'Postscript: Towards a Radical Eclecticism', suggested the end of this phase when it was published in early 1981.

POSTMODERN CLASSICISM

Postmodern Classicism – the style that is arguably most popularly aligned with postmodern architecture – began with the May/June 1980 *Ɒ* Profile of that name. A rare editorial by Papadakis noted that 'Investigating the recent work of numerous architects in America, Europe and Japan, Jencks identifies a trend towards Classicism within Post-Modern architecture, a tendency further demonstrated at the Venice Biennale.'[8] Jencks was hopeful for this new trend, arguing that 'In the past year there has been a convergence of styles within Post-Modernism, a convergence towards a manner which could be called classical.' He continued, 'the largest movement is Post-Modern Classicism, a free style which, we may hope, will continue to be lively and will not become still-born.'[9] The origin of Jencks's classification of this style was found in the first Venice Architecture Biennale, held in 1980 on the theme of 'The Presence of the Past'. Jencks provided 123 pages of example buildings by American architects such as Moore, Venturi & Rauch, Stern and Graves, as well as newer, more international cannon fodder such as Ricardo Bofill, Morphosis and Jeremy Dixon.

In November 1980, Papadakis produced a simple, folded black-and-white 'News Supplement' that championed Postmodernism's successes. The second supplement of January 1981 reflected on the Biennale and identified the emergence of two main tendencies – Classicism and Eclecticism – noting that 'the relevance of history and, more specifically, Classicism, to current architecture is not in doubt'.[10] These two tendencies formed the basis of two *Ɒ* Profiles in 1982. The January/February issue, guest-edited by Jencks and called *Free-Style Classicism*, followed the wider, Eclectic line, 'with the epithet "free style" demanding a more generous interpretation of the Classical tenets and a flexibility in cultural concepts as vital as that witnessed daily in linguistic and semantic intention'.[11] This was a hybrid, Postmodern Classicism whose architects – mainly from the US and Japan – had tried Modernism and rejected it. May/June's edition, *Classicism is Not a Style*, which was guest-edited by Demetri Porphyrios, aimed to 'look at classicism only for the lessons it has to teach us about the nature of tectonic and architecture discourse and about the distance that separates them'.[12] This was a traditional, pure Neoclassicism whose architects, mainly from Europe, had rejected Modernism before trying it. The one thing that united the two positions, however, was an agreement that Modernism had failed.

Ɒ Post-Modern History,
January 1978

Within a year, Jencks had already updated his book and Academy published the second edition, promoted by this *Ɒ* issue.

Ɒ Free-Style Classicism,
January/February 1982

The first of two *Ɒ* issues exploring Postmodern Classicism, which argued for a contemporary eclectic style through texts by OM Ungers, Arata Isozaki and Charles Moore among others. The cover shows James Stirling and Michael Wilford's design for the Clore Gallery extension at Tate Britain.

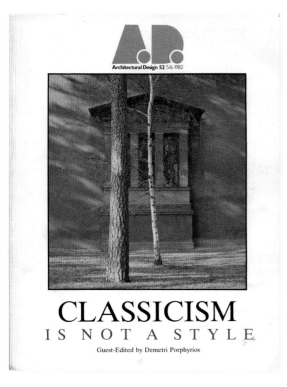

Classicism is Not a Style,
May/June 1982

In this issue, guest-editor Demetri Porphyrios rallied
against eclecticism and viewing postmodern architecture
as a language, and argued for a purer form of classical
architecture based on tectonics.

Designing a House,
September/October 1985

This ∆ was devoted to Charles Jencks's own house,
designed with Terry Farrell. The same year Academy
Editions published Jencks's book-length description
of the house's complex symbolic meanings: *Towards
a Symbolic Architecture: The Thematic House.*

NEO-VERNACULAR

∆'s 'Neo-Vernacular' phase of Postmodernism commenced
with the publication of the fourth edition of *The Language
of Post-Modern Architecture* in early 1984. ∆ marked the
occasion by publishing a conversation between Jencks and
Papadakis that ended with a clear affirmation that: 'The
first stage of Post-Modernism is complete.'[13] Although this
phase included the publication of the fifth edition of Jencks's
book three years later, it also witnessed the cooling of the
relationship between author and publisher. Jencks continued
to contribute to ∆, but only guest-edited a single Profile,
jointly with Terry Farrell, on the design of his own house.[14]

In the late 1980s, ∆ continued to promote
Postmodernism, but with more of an emphasis on the ideas
of Porphyrios and the Krier brothers. The first Academy
Symposium, at the Tate Gallery in London, was held in
October 1987 on the subject of Postmodernism. The
proceedings were published as a Jencks book and written up
briefly in the following ∆ with the conclusion that 'through
a number of approaches and with heated debate, a viable
new aesthetic is taking hold'.[15] This new tactic of holding
high-profile symposia and publishing the results proved
popular, and the following symposium introduced the next
postmodern fashion to architecture: one that completely
disproved the previous symposium's conclusion.

DECONSTRUCTIVISM

In 1988, Academy in London and the Museum of Modern
Art (MoMA) in New York competed to be the first to deliver
Deconstructivist architecture to the world. Jencks brought
news from America of the birth of this new architectural
movement, and Papadakis responded quickly by setting up
a symposium at the Tate Gallery on Saturday 26 March, the
proceedings of which formed the basis of the next ∆.[16]
The MoMA 'Deconstructivist Architecture' show did not
start until 23 June, by which time the ∆ *Deconstruction*
Profile was already available, showing almost exactly the
same group of architects: Coop Himmelb(l)au, Frank Gehry,
Zaha Hadid, Peter Eisenman, OMA and Bernard Tschumi.
∆ had already published a number of high-quality Profiles
on Russian Constructivism, guest-edited by Catherine Cooke,
which were highly influential on Deconstructivist architects.
Constructivism's abstract, industrial aesthetic of the early
20th-century Russian avant-garde was combined with Jacques
Derrida's ideas of Deconstruction, which had recently been
introduced to architectural discourse. The ∆ Profile borrowed
its name from this latter literary movement and became an
instant bestseller. Two sequels[17] duly appeared in the same
format of dense theoretical articles on Deconstructivism
(as the movement became known in architecture), followed
by seductive drawings and photographs of models and the
occasional building.

This fourth and final phase of the Jencks/Papadakis ∆
era ended in early 1991 with the publication of Jencks's
sixth edition of *The Language of Post-Modern Architecture*
(the final edition published by Academy) and two ∆ Profiles
hailing both the death of Postmodernism and, by implication,
its success as a style. The first, *Post-Modernism on Trial*
(November/December 1990),[18] was written in a retrospective
mood following the usual formula of several dense theoretical

and polemical articles followed by a number of exemplary buildings featured in high gloss and full colour. Introducing the Profile, Jencks wrote: 'Now that Post-Modern architecture has triumphed around the world, many people have declared it dead. This, the fate of all successful movements, is something to be celebrated.'[19] Its death was blamed on too rapid a commercial complicity with corporations like Disney, for whom Michael Graves had designed a headquarters in California sporting seven giant caryatid dwarves looking more ridiculous than ironic. The second Profile, *Post-Modern Triumphs in London* (May/June 1991),[20] was Jencks's △D swansong where he consciously constructed a canon of postmodern architecture in London as a kind of legacy.

'NOW THAT POST-MODERN ARCHITECTURE HAS TRIUMPHED AROUND THE WORLD, MANY PEOPLE HAVE DECLARED IT DEAD. THIS, THE FATE OF ALL SUCCESSFUL MOVEMENTS, IS SOMETHING TO BE CELEBRATED.'

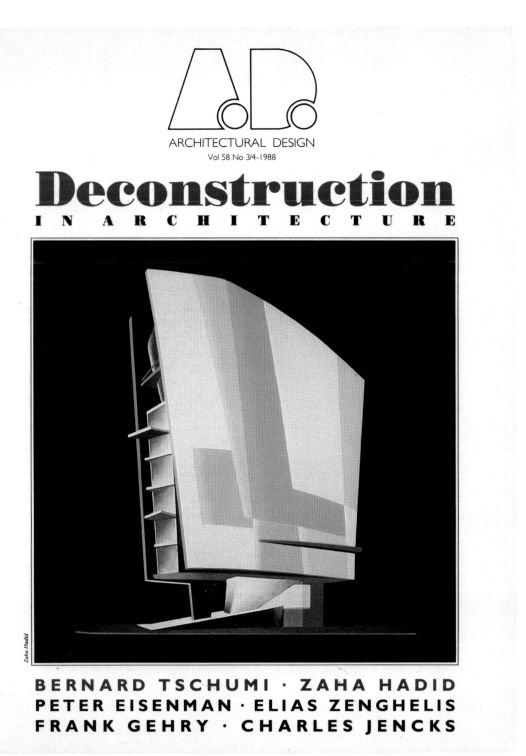

△D ARCHITECTURAL DESIGN
Vol 58 No 3/4-1988

Deconstruction
IN ARCHITECTURE

Zaha Hadid

BERNARD TSCHUMI · ZAHA HADID
PETER EISENMAN · ELIAS ZENGHELIS
FRANK GEHRY · CHARLES JENCKS

△D *Deconstruction in Architecture*, March/April 1988

Deconstructivism, a combination of a rediscovered Constructivist architecture and the theory of Jacques Derrida, signalled a new direction for Postmodernism. Thanks to a tip-off by Jencks, Academy beat New York's Museum of Modern Art (MoMA) to a symposium and resulting publication showing almost the same architects.

AD Post-Modernism on Trial,
November/December 1990

These two issues of *AD* represent the end of Jencks's
and Academy's promotion of the movement. Jencks
had tried Postmodernism and – unsurprisingly –
found that it had succeeded, but had come to an end.
He therefore claimed victory for the movement and
consciously constructed a canon of architects.

AD Post-Modern Triumphs in London,
May/June 1991

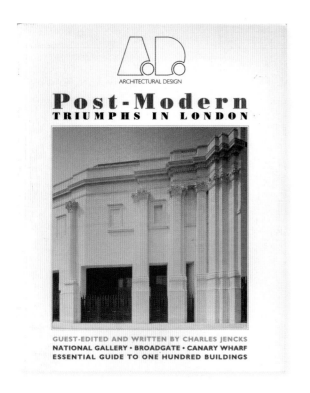

MULTIFORM

For many architects, Postmodernism was always a dirty
word. Jencks's PhD supervisor, Reyner Banham, for example,
famously called it 'building in drag',[21] and *AD*'s friendly rival,
the *Architectural Review*, never accepted or legitimised it.
After Papadakis sold Academy to the German publisher VCH
in 1991 and left at the end of the following year, *AD* ploughed
a new furrow with digital computation. But Postmodernism
never disappeared completely. The boy band of architecture,
FAT (Fashion Architecture Taste) was established in the mid-
1990s and became an antidote to 'good taste' from the get-go.
A number of small, fun, clever and provocatively iconoclastic
works appeared culminating (from the media point of view
at least) with the *AD Radical Post-Modernism* issue a decade
ago, guest-edited by FAT and Jencks, alongside a new book by
Jencks – also published by Wiley, which acquired *AD* in 1996 –
reflecting on the movement.[22] It was time for Postmodernism
itself to be historicised.

Looking to the present, we might detect certain stylistic
similarities to the baby-boomer strains of Postmodernism
from the 1980s, but the medium (which Marshall McLuhan
famously equated to the message) that the latest generation
of postmodern protagonists/Multiformers use is social
media. If mediation was a core strategy of Modernism,
Postmodernism made it an art form. But if Jencks were
promoting his movement today, it would be on Instagram
rather than in *AD*, enabling him to even more quickly update
his bubble diagrams with his 'genius for categorisation'[23]
rendered in hashtags rather than 'isms'.

Instagram is the natural home for Generation-Y
Postmodernists, those who were born after the original
movement and therefore were not immunised against it like
FAT would have been. It is where influencers like artist and
designer Adam Nathaniel Furman (34.7k followers at the time
of writing) so effectively promote their work. The legitimation
rendered by the cultural capital bestowed upon work by a
magazine like *AD* means less in the online world of 'likes' and
'retweets' where a message, or 'meme', can be sent around the
world in seconds and going viral is considered a fleeting mark
of success, like appearing on the cover of a magazine might
once have been.

POSTMODERNISM NEVER
DISAPPEARED COMPLETELY.
THE BOY BAND OF
ARCHITECTURE, FAT (FASHION
ARCHITECTURE TASTE)
WAS ESTABLISHED IN THE
MID-1990S AND BECAME AN
ANTIDOTE TO 'GOOD TASTE'
FROM THE GET-GO

A whole new taste regime emerges on Instagram where facadism and surface are taken to the next level. Here you can find a nostalgia for Ettore Sottsass and the Memphis Group, for example, in the work of Camille Walala (153k followers – see the interview with her on pp 84–91 of this issue) or Morag Myerscough (34.3k followers). Their sunny designs of primary colours and primitive shapes are unapologetically joyful, as are those of Yinka Ilori (29.1k followers – see pp 118–27), whose Dulwich Pavilion in London of 2019 was not so much functional as just fun.

A more serious, knowing humour based on historical reference can be found in architects like Studio MUTT (4.2k followers – see pp 26–31) with their overscaled dividers at the Ordnance Pavilion in England's Lake District National Park (2018) that recalls Frank Gehry in Los Angeles circa 1991, or Space Popular (8k followers – see pp 76–83), whose Brick Vault House in Valencia (2019) is very Stirling Staatsgalerie of 1984. Space Popular take Multiform beyond style, though, with their interest in integrating digital technology into physical space, such as in their 'Freestyle: Architectural Adventures in Mass Media' exhibition at the Royal Institute of British Architects (RIBA) in London (2020), which integrated virtual reality with physical models against a brightly patterned backdrop, while questioning the whole concept of style. Which all goes to show that Postmodernism never died – it just finds new media to resist the false imperative of the Zeitgeist.[24] ⌂

Notes
1. Reinhold Martin, *Utopia's Ghost: Architecture and Postmodernism, Again*, University of Minnesota Press (Minneapolis, MN and London), 2010, p xii.
2. Charles Jencks, 'The Rise of Post-Modern Architecture', *Architectural Association Quarterly*, 7.4, 1975, pp 3–14.
3. Charles Jencks and George Baird (eds), *Meaning in Architecture*, Barrie & Rockliff (London), 1969.
4. Charles Jencks, *The Language of Post-Modern Architecture*, Academy Editions (London), 1977.
5. Charles Jencks, 'Isozaki and Radical Eclecticism', ⌂ Profile: *Arata Isozaki*, January 1977, p 48.
6. *Ibid*, p 46.
7. Haig Beck, 'Contents: ⌂ Profiles 4 – Post-Modernism', ⌂ *Post-Modernism*, April 1977, p 239.
8. Andreas Papadakis, 'Editorial', ⌂ *Post-Modern Classicism*, May/June 1980, p 68.
9. Charles Jencks, 'Introduction', in *ibid*, p 5.
10. JG, 'Classicism or Eclecticism?', ⌂ *Supplement*, January 1981, unpaginated.
11. Andreas Papadakis, 'Editorial: Classicism or Eclecticism?', ⌂ *Free-Style Classicism*, January/February 1982, p 4.
12. Demetri Porphyrios, 'Introduction', ⌂ *Classicism is Not a Style*, May/June 1982, p 5.
13. Andreas Papadakis and Charles Jencks, 'Post-Modern Classicism – the Synthesis: An Interview with Charles Jencks', ⌂ *British Architecture*, March/April 1984, p 63.
14. Charles Jencks (ed), ⌂ *Designing a House*, September/October 1985.
15. 'Post-Modernism at the Tate: New Trends in Art & Architecture', ⌂ *Engineering and Architecture*, November/December 1987, p II.
16. Charles Jencks (ed), ⌂ *Deconstruction in Architecture*, March/April 1988.
17. ⌂ *Deconstruction II*, January/February 1989; and ⌂ *Deconstruction III*, September/October 1990.
18. Charles Jencks (ed), ⌂ *Post-Modernism on Trial*, November/December 1990.
19. Charles Jencks, 'Death for Rebirth', in *ibid*, p 6.
20. Charles Jencks (ed), ⌂ *Post-Modern Triumphs in London*, May/June 1991.
21. Reyner Banham, 'A Black Box: The Secret Profession of Architecture', in Mary Banham *et al* (eds), *A Critic Writes: Essays by Reyner Banham*, University of California Press (Berkeley, CA), 1996, p 293.
22. Charles Jencks *et al* (eds), ⌂ *Radical Post-Modernism*, September/October (no 5), 2011; Charles Jencks, *The Story of Post-Modernism: Five Decades of Architecture*, John Wiley & Sons (London), 2011.
23. Andreas Papadakis, 'Abstract Representation', ⌂ *Abstract Representation*, July/August 1983, p 49.
24. Jencks dedicated his *Story of Post-Modernism* book 'to all those who have resisted the false imperative of the zeitgeist'.

⌂ *Radical Post-Modernism*, September/October 2011

A new interest in Postmodernism emerged about a decade ago. This ⌂ issue, guest-edited by Jencks and Sam Jacob, Charles Holland and Sean Griffiths of FAT (Fashion Architecture Taste), signified the beginning of the historicisation of Postmodernism itself.

Dirk Somers

PLURALI
URBAN *LAND*

Bovenbouw architectuur,
Renovation of 19th-century
buildings for residential use,
Leysstraat, Antwerp, Belgium,
2016

The refurbishment project in Antwerp's main
shopping street built further on the rich stack
of neo-Renaissance motifs and figures of the
late-19th-century elevations.

SM AND THE SCAPE

TOWARDS A STRATEGIC *ECLECTICISM*

Alison and Peter Smithson,
Economist Building,
London,
1964

The Smithsons' enigmatic building, situated
in London's historic St James's district,
shows how to transcend the false discussion
between harmony and pluralism.

Whilst Multiform has achieved a certain acceptance as a way of combating the so-called New London Vernacular's contextual architecture, there are still many other aspects of urbanism it does not necessarily address, particularly within the public realm. The cityscape is often left out of the debate where buildings risk becoming simply self-referential objects. **Dirk Somers**, manager and founder of Antwerp's Bovenbouw architectuur, argues for a reconsideration and posits successful precedents that balance convention with surprise.

The postmodern revival debate in the UK is intriguing, because it is not raging on the Continent. In Europe nobody denies us the use of historical references, colourful combinations of materials or round windows. In any pluralistic society there will always be supporters and opponents of any stylistic manoeuvre, but there is undeniably a market for richly layered buildings and therefore little reason to try to kick down doors that are already open.

One of the targets of the debate in the UK is what some see as the consensus that has emerged around the more established contextual architecture, which is perceived to be dull and generic.[1] The enemy has already been given a name in London: New London Vernacular. Everyone knows that labels are a well-functioning poison in the cultural debate. Architects always tend to shun the sticky glue of a group label. It eats the uniqueness and dynamic image of a practice. But is the New London Vernacular disease really so malicious that it must be combated so fanatically?

These stylistic, formal discussions eventually come together physically in the urban landscape, and that landscape does not seem to benefit much from the postmodern revival for the time being. The urban landscape was already the big loser of the entire modern architectural debate. The streets and squares of the city swung from left to right throughout the 20th century until they no longer knew who to listen to. The Postmodernism of the 1970s and 1980s put the street back on the agenda with varying degrees of success. But today, unlike the postmodern architecture debate, the urban landscape debate has yet to begin a solid revival.

Now that Britain is once again discussing the value of Postmodernism, it must urgently expand the discussion beyond questions of style and debate the urban landscape again. That debate is worth much more than the fashionable delirium of pastel and concave. It does not matter whether a building is labelled New London Vernacular or something else. More important is the urban landscape it contributes to, which is where the success of a building should be judged. Two measures that can be used to weigh that success fall under the headings of 'composition' and 'mannerism'.

Composition

Today's city is undeniably pluralistic. Those who try to formally suppress that fact are quickly dismissed as nostalgic. At first sight, that strict judgement against nostalgic repression is true. Why can't we accept the city as a space as chaotic as the social debate and all its actors? Why should architects and administrations be concerned with suppressing the multitude of expressions that characterise our society?

Those who think a little harder quickly unmask the deception of this kind of rhetoric. The dilemma between genuine but messy pluralism and feigned harmonious urbanity frames the problem of the contemporary urban landscape as a false choice. Why can't the urban landscape be pluralistic and harmonious at the same time? Is there not an objective basis that can reconcile our desire for harmony with our desire for diversity? Does social pluralism imply that we have to undo all architectural shackles and embrace stylistic anarchy? Such a position could be seen as equivalent to the rejection of the importance of civility and good social relations.

Pursuing this analogy between urban landscape and civil society further, we might define a healthy society as one that continuously seeks an optimal balance between individual freedom and public interest. The urban landscape symbolises that search for balance. In the midst of that amalgam of disputes and processes, some argue for more freedom and others for more discipline. That is part of the continuous search for agreement. Just as in the political spectrum, everyone on the urban playing field, more often implicitly than explicitly, advocates their own idea about spatial order. There is no reasonable person who defends total urban chaos, or vice versa, the return to a purely classical city.

Architects like to invoke artistic freedom when they are losing in the style debate. But the argument of artistic and expressive freedom rests on a shaky analogy with the artist's practice. In contrast to the visual arts, architecture rarely operates in its own space, but almost always in a shared space. Urban architecture, unlike the villa in the forest, functions as part of a conglomerate. Architecture can therefore only rely on the artistic freedom of expression if it can demonstrate that this freedom is in balance with the presence of nearby buildings. It goes without saying that we expect more discipline from a row house in a historic street than from a pavilion in a suburban park.

When references to Alison and Peter Smithson's Economist Building in London reappear in a bundle for a design review board or a competition procedure, it is difficult to suppress an affable smile. Completed in 1964, it must be the most popular reference of a design that gives a powerfully idiosyncratic shape to a series of new ideas and yet manages to complement the composition of the street in a meaningful way. The conglomerate deviates from its environment typologically and tectonically, but compensates for this through material and compositional operations that generate interesting points of contact.

Of the many contemporary design proposals that used the Economist Building as a reference, none achieves the same level of tension between individuality and assimilation. But that is not necessary. The Economist Building is an enigma, which is repeatedly referred to – whether consciously or not – as a way of transcending the false choice between harmony and pluralism.

Composition is a difficult field of knowledge that we are all somehow aware of. We say things like 'this works' and 'this doesn't work', we talk about heavy and light, about appropriate and inappropriate, about inviting and repulsive. We look for words to say what our senses have long told us about the multitude of stimuli that a building sends to us. The compositional view disconnects the building from its cultural or ethical merits. That is problematic, but also relevant. Anyone who knows nothing about the Smithsons can still appreciate how the Economist Building works in the street. That has everything to do with scale, continuation and detailing, and nothing to do with structuralism or Team X.

Of course, you cannot separate the phenomenological success of the building from its intellectual roots and aspirations, but we still see here how the success of ideas and the success of buildings keep an important distance from each other. When we talk about the successful interplay of buildings, we should keep the ideas and the rhetoric at a distance. All too often good ideas are used to promote bad buildings; ideas and buildings are not always each other's best friends.

This discord also explains why many postmodern buildings perform worse in the urban landscape than Modernist buildings. Intellectually we should assume that a postmodern building always wins the contextual battle, but in practice this turns out to be wrong. Composition is a more reliable gauge than ideology in our experience of the urban landscape. The formal and material relationships weigh much more in our appreciation of a building than the rhetoric, principles and world of ideas that lie behind the design.

Mannerism

'Composition' is an imperfect term to describe the plastic and physical coherence of the urban landscape. The field of knowledge regarding the visual and material experience of the city does not have a conclusive name, although there are a number of studies that illustrate its legitimacy.[2] But the Achilles' heel of such a visual approach to the urban landscape is the exclusion of the cultural and social aspects of architecture. The urban landscape is much more than a complex, ever-developing sculpture, hence the need for a second criterion to speak of a benign urban environment.

Robert Venturi and Denise Scott Brown's book *Architecture as Signs and Systems: For a Mannerist Time* (2004) repeats many of their previous insights and positions, but also visibly enjoys looking back from 50 years of accumulated perspective. In the book, the architects navigate the space between architectural freedom and discipline: 'The architect who cares not at all for context is a bore, the architect who cares only for context is a bore.'[3] Mannerism, as in their previous publications, remains a key concept that reflects the need for a versatile mindset, away from the exclusive determinism of the Modernist architect. The mannerism that Venturi and Scott Brown aim for is the discipline and empathy to think inclusively without losing sight of the pursuit of architectural consistency.

Mannerism becomes even more explicitly inclusive in the context of the elegant studies that Venturi, Scott Brown and Steven Izenour mounted of the seemingly most vulgar environments in *Learning from Las Vegas* (1972). Here, they effortlessly bridge the gap between an apparently snobbish label like mannerism and the social involvement of urban sociologists like Jane Jacobs or Herbert Gans.[4]

Venturi and Scott Brown use mannerism as a label for a jovial design culture that embraces social commitment and an inclusive view of the world. This open mind is central to their discourse on city and architecture, but they do add the compositional concept of 'inflection'. They realised that messy vitality of the pluralistic city must boil down to a complex work in which all parts are convincingly connected to each other. Inflection indicates how all parts of a building refer to each other, thereby contributing to the success and coherence of the entire composition.

But inflection at the building level means little if the urban-planning scale only causes chaos and disruption. At city scale, the desire for inflection applies just as much as at a building scale. The desire for pluralism and inclusion should therefore not be misunderstood for an urban-planning laissez-faire. Venturi and Scott Brown's mannerism longs for a city that is unpredictable and diverse, without giving up the intense dialogue between buildings.

Venturi, Scott Brown and Associates,
Sainsbury Wing of the National Gallery,
London,
1991

The Sainsbury Wing is an example of a successful postmodern move, offering exciting complexity without useless provocation.

Strategic Eclecticism

In Bovenbouw's architectuur's work, the compositional concerns about the urban landscape and the sociocultural interweaving of mannerism merge into what we call a strategic eclecticism. Venturi and Scott Brown indirectly provide a compositional argument for such an eclecticism when stating 'if all is exception, exception is not interesting anymore'.[5]

The bidding and accumulation of architectural ambitions increasingly diverges the urban landscape. As a result, the clutter of today's city compels us to an even more radical spread between discipline and ingenuity. In the contemporary city we need to avoid unnecessary exceptions and embrace everything exceptional. To avoid total entropy and flattening, we have to employ a radical form of empathy.

To avoid total entropy and flattening, we have to employ a radical form of empathy

Bovenbouw architectuur,
Renovation of 19th-century
buildings for residential use,
Leysstraat, Antwerp, Belgium,
2016

In this refurbishment the consistency between exterior and interior is strengthened by extending the eclectic design approach inwards.

Bovenbouw architectuur,
School extension in Edegem,
Antwerp,
Belgium,
2017

The blockwork of the new kindergarten building
cheerfully contributes to an old kinked street made
up of red-brick building.

This empathy leads to stylistic promiscuity in Bovenbouw's oeuvre. Brutalist tropes suit brutalist campuses, such as the practice's 2009 garage and storage hangar extension to the 1970s-built Destelheide Learning Centre in Dworp, south of Brussels (2009), where the interplay of rough concrete and topography characterise both the historical, brutalist layout and the new intervention, or in a neo-Renaissance context, such as the 2016 refurbishment of three 19th-century buildings in Antwerp's central street, Leysstraat, for residential use, in an area that had become purely a shopping district, include references to those architectural features on the interior as well as the facade; gothic town halls see reinterpretations of gothic plasticity; and in Modernist offices inspiration is taken from Modernist gestures.

This empathy also extends to the way Bovenbouw relates new buildings to the existing urban fabric, for example in the family house in Brussels (2019) where a blind bay is introduced to the front of the house to allude to protruding bay windows – a common feature in the city's housing – or the viewing tower that the practice and David Kohn Architects are adding to the Beguinage in Hasselt, Belgium. The disappearance of the monumental church in the centre of the convent triggers the introduction of the brick tower, restoring the morphological balance of the site.

Sometimes a weak context compels unruly behaviour, and Bovenbouw looks for pit where the context is saltless, or for cooling where overheating occurs. Such indulgent versatility may seem libertine, but it is just the opposite. Strategic eclecticism is alive with empathy and fully enjoying the hopeless struggle against the flattening disorder of today's city. Strategic eclecticism is about stylistic diversity, intelligently applied. ⚿

Notes
1. Adam Nathaniel Furman, 'Outrage: "There Is A Silent Agreement In Contemporary British Architecture: You May Deploy Ornament, But Never Too Much"', *Architectural Review*, 24 March 2017: www.architectural-review.com/essays/campaigns/outrage/outrage-there-is-a-silent-agreement-in-contemporary-british-architecture-you-may-deploy-ornament-but-never-too-much/10018361.article.
2. For example: Pierre von Meiss, *Elements of Architecture* (1970); Steen Eiler Rasmussen, *Experiencing Architecture* (1959); Christopher Alexander, Sara Ishikawa and Murray Silverstein, *A Pattern Language* (1977); Rudolf Arnheim, *The Dynamics of Architectural Form* (1977); Howard Robertson, *The Principles of Architectural Composition* (1955); and A Trystan Edwards, *Architectural Style* (1926).
3. Robert Venturi and Denise Scott Brown, *Architecture as Signs and Systems: For a Mannerist Time,* Belknap Press of Harvard University Press (Boston, MA), 2004, p 177.
4. Robert Venturi, Denise Scott Brown and Steven Izenour, *Learning From Las Vegas: The Forgotten Symbolism of Architectural Form*, The MIT Press (Boston, MA), 1972, p 115.
5. Venturi and Scott Brown, *Architecture as Signs and Systems, op cit*, p 212.

Bovenbouw architectuur and
David Kohn Architects (DKA),
Viewing tower,
Beguinage,
Hasselt, Belgium,
due for completion 2022

Reconstructing the unexpected: the viewing tower reintroduces a monumental brick figure as a substitution for the ruined church that was bombed during the Second World War.

#ARCHIT

RACKZ, SHACKZ AND THE OPP

ECTUREZ

ORTUNITIES *IN* BETWEEN

CAN,
HCKNEY HSE,
Church Walk,
Stoke Newington,
London,
construction to begin 2021

The front elevation looks to combine
the aesthetics of the rest of the
buildings on the street.

A mock tudor/gothic/classical clusterf*ck of a toy shop in Barmouth, North Wales, provided the eureka moment for CAN's first building commission. CAN had been appointed to design the joint Lomax Studio (2018) down a scrappy industrial mews in New Cross, London, for two very different artists: a sculptor working on large-scale metalworks and a printmaker creating delicate art books. Alongside the practical issues of providing two functionally opposed spaces in one open-plan studio, the practice was working through ideas of how one building could visually represent the opposing aesthetics of the two artists.

Mat Barnes is a director of London-based architectural practice CAN. He believes ill-conceived, expedient parts of cities – the bits that are unplanned and left to their own devices – are fecund breeding grounds for formal and material innovation. These are places of happy collisions of architectural elements that are ripe for further architectural insertions and experiments. Here he presents some of his practice's work in such contexts.

Toy shop,
Barmouth,
North Wales,
2016

An example of several architectural styles combined into one architectural form.

Steptoes & Sons
architectural salvage yard,
Camberwell,
London,
2020

An example of a Shack(z), a building made from to-hand materials with no formal considerations to aesthetics or architectural harmony.

The toy shop was a condensed and purified form of an ongoing interest in architecturally incoherent buildings or streets, made from a mash-up of materials and architectural styles, referred to as #Architecturez in the practice. They are the Lolspeak of urban fabric: the grammatically incorrect architectural leftovers. #Architecturez generally fit into two categories crudely termed 'Shackz' and 'Rackz'. Shackz are standalone buildings and the most primitive, created through necessity and often from whatever material is to hand. They are the workshops, the sheds, the timber yards, and are made from adapted signs, secondhand windows, car doors and scrap metal. Often constructed without planning permission, they survive and exist mainly in areas where planning restrictions are loose, enforcement is lacking, and there is an absence of discussion about the physical fabric of place.

Rackz are the streets and groups of buildings that have no dominant architectural style, fenestration rhythm or materiality. The visually competing buildings have little relationship to one another and revel in their difference. Rackz are rare in London, but usually happen when the development of the street is relatively new, no dominant 'context' has been established, and the conservation area overlords do not have control. Development precedent for Rackz is often created by a collection of Shackz located along back alleys or ex-industrial land that have become viable sites for housing as land values reach a certain threshold. The plots are generally developed by existing private freeholders for sale rather than occupancy. This profit-led, bit-part approach leads to an incoherent

architectural response as sites are developed separately to different briefs and budgets with little planning policy or design guidance. This incoherence is fertile ground for more adventurous and experimental architectural proposals that would be quickly refused in areas suffering from a dominant 'context' and a local 'good taste' brigade.

#Architecturez embody the most primitive version of the 'ad hoc' explored by Charles Jencks and Nathan Silver in *Adhocism: The Case for Improvisation*, originally published in 1972.[1] They are built with a general and loose approach rather than a tight and systematic one. If they have planning permission they are only constrained by the basic rules of massing and overlooking and not by the tighter rules governing appearance and materiality imposed in 'higher-quality' contexts. They are built of 'to-hand' materials (reused or the cheapest from the local building merchant) using the simplest of techniques permissible by building control (if indeed they consult building control at all). This limits their response to the immediate locale, reacting to the physical parameters of the site and availability of cheap local materials.

DEATH TO HETEROGENEITY
The current planning regime and continuing commercialisation of land and home is decreasing the opportunity for, and prevalence of, these ad-hoc #Architecturez, which help provide crucial test beds

Viaduct Place,
Bethnal Green,
London,
2020

An example of a Rack(z), a collection of buildings and Shackz built in an ad hoc and incoherent way. They have no dominant architectural style.

for emerging architectural ideas. They also add to the variety of difference in cities and represent their innate social contradictions, creating a rich urban fabric, key to the vibrancy of a city like London. As soon as the regeneration carpet-bomber homes in on the next 'area of opportunity', Shackz are under threat and opportunity for new Rackz diminishes. Developers swoop in and buy up all the viable land, covering it in blocks styled in the New London Vernacular. As house prices increase, residents become more and more concerned with the effect residual #Architecturez have on their house values and become more vocal in championing homogeny. This homogeny is the arch-nemesis of the ad hoc, scrappy #Architecturez and their experimental architectural offspring.

The biggest hurdle to any new 'style' ('Multiform' included) is conservative taste, which Jencks and Silver suggested was the reason the hybrid style of Adhocism remained a small trend.[2] This conservative taste is particularly strong in the UK and manifests itself as contextualist-driven planning policy. A desperate desire to blend in – 'only speak when you are spoken to, boy!' – but only if the context is deemed to be of high-enough quality, which usually means it has to have been built before the Second World War.

DESIGNING THE UN-DESIGNED
These leftover bits on the fringes of taste and acceptability provided an unlikely design approach for CAN on the Lomax Studio project, as well as a later proposal, the HCKNEY HSE (2020).

Lomax Studio is located down a rough, barely walkable industrial mews in New Cross littered with Shackz: garages, industrial sheds and workshops. How do you respond to the un-considered? The normal approach is to forget the 'unworthy' context and go hardcore on whatever style is your thing. The Barmouth toy shop gave CAN a different solution: the idea of condensing the difference of a Rack(z) into a single building. This mash-up (or Multiform?) approach perfectly matched the brief; this was a studio for two very different artists who have visually opposed outputs and require very different working environments. Added to this, the plot was nearly double the width of the rest of the plots on the mews, so a large single-material building would have dwarfed the other Shackz. The studio appears as two – externally matching the scale of the other Shackz while functioning as one studio internally. The materials were chosen for their inherent difference: glossy versus matte, smooth versus rough, light versus dark, crisp versus fuzzy. The detailing continues this opposition with finer ornamental elements used in the tiled volume, and clunky off-the-shelf industrial elements used in the larger volume.

HCKNEY HSE is located on a Rack(z) in North London; a mix of Shackz, industrial buildings, newly developed housing and architectural experiments. CAN was commissioned to reimagine a dilapidated newbuild from 2006, and proposed retaining the main structure of the house, but totally rethinking the street-facing facade. Whereas Lomax Studio represents its occupants with its two unique volumes, HCKNEY HSE condenses the whole smörgåsbord of the

CAN,
Lomax Studio,
New Cross,
London,
2018

The two distinct volumes of the studio responded to the scale and incoherence of the context. They also represented the different practices of the two artists working in the studio.

Context for CAN's HCKNEY HSE,
Church Walk, Stoke Newington,
London,
construction to begin 2021

The street is a perfect example of a Rack(z), a combination of buildings of various uses, styles, ages and architectural consideration and experimentation.

Rack(z) into one facade: the flattening of the whole street into a screen's depth. A singular approach felt too expected and ill-fitting. Coherent architecture on an incoherent street did not make sense. The result was a bricolage facade encompassing the industrial, the ornate, the ecclesiastical and the budget, arranged to exaggerate the qualities of the other.

The context for both projects called for something that riffed off the lack of homogeneity: an abundance of materials and ideas smashed together; a rejection of the fetishisation of handmade bricks and muted material palettes that have become the mainstay of London's 'good taste/better than you' architecture scene; a counter to British conservatism and a twisted inversion of London's rampant contextualism. What could be more contextual than smashing all the buildings on the street into one?! It is also a reaction to the aesthetic restraints present on CAN's other projects, an opportunity to test the waters and widen the architectural conversation.

FAMILIAL **TRAITS**
The common 'broken up' (Multiform?) aesthetic of Lomax Studio and HCKNEY HSE has compositional similarities with the collected object (or still life) aesthetic of some postmodern buildings of the late 1980s and early 1990s, such as Arata Isozaki's Team Disney Building in Orlando (1991) and Frank Gehry's Winton Guest House on Lake Minnetonka, Minnesota (1987). These are the final flourishes of that movement and are very firmly placed in eclecticism,

sourcing ideas and references from far and wide. However, their lineage can be traced back to Adhocism via works such as Gehry's own house in Santa Monica (1978), which reflects a loose approach using the everyday materials of its locale. CAN's work could similarly be read as an evolution of the pure Adhocism represented in #Architecturez, the considered version of the unconsidered. The practice's output may well evolve into a similar eclecticism should Multiform become an accepted architectural currency (anything can happen these days). The battle over conservative tastes and contextualism could be won.

For this to happen some of London needs to remain scrappy. #Architecturez not only provide fertile ground for Multiform experiments, but can also provide a compositional framework for their design. Their continued loss risks the wave of Multiform being resigned to Instagram hashtags and the rear gardens of an enlightened few, never to be experienced by the public at large. There may be some hope found in the increased demand for reused or to-hand materials needed to tackle the climate emergency resulting in a more patchwork (or ad-hoc) urban fabric. Could the circular economy become the unlikely bedfellow of Multiform? ⚹

Notes
1. Charles Jencks and Nathan Silver, *Adhocism: The Case for Improvisation*, The MIT Press (Cambridge, MA), expanded and updated edition, 2013, p 16.
2. *Ibid*, p viii.

Gehry Partners,
Winton Guest House,
Hudson Valley, New York,
2015

Originally constructed in 1987 on Lake Minnetonka, the guest house was donated to the University of St Thomas in Minnesota in 2007, where it stood until it was auctioned off and moved again in 2015. It is an example of the broken-form aesthetic popular in the last Postmodern period; more sculptural and with less references than most Postmodernism that came before it.

EXPLORING, BUILDING, COMPLETING

Amin Taha is Chairman of London architectural office Groupwork and is no stranger to architectural controversy. The practice's buildings are often highly original and predicated on a thorough historical, contextual and collaborative research approach that goes far beyond the simple binary logics of ill-conceived planning dogma. New design protocols are developed for each project and these evolve organically as the scheme progresses.

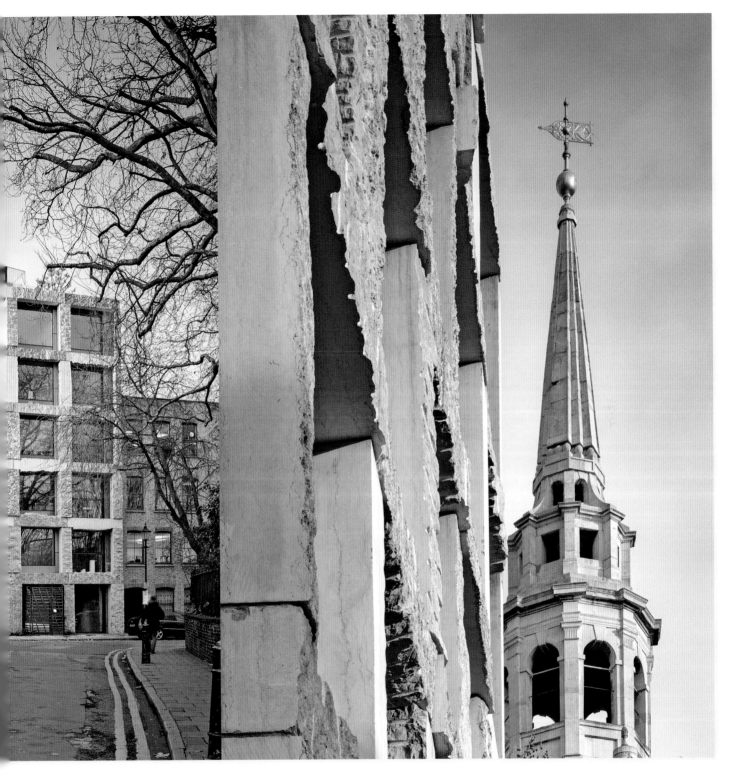

Groupwork,
15 Clerkenwell Close,
London,
2017

above left: A tectonic limestone exoskeleton rejects the 1970s and 1980s neighbours of suspended half-brick stretcher-bond skins – and instead offers a pedagogic tectonic narrative of the buildings that stood on the site until the early 19th century.

above right: Piles of loadbearing limestone allude to local archaeology but raise new questions about architectural heritage today.

Why should a building look as it does? Why select one material over another? Why assemble them so? Does the result need to mean anything at all? These questions are perennial ones of artifice. All building materials have structural properties that are as immutable as the force of gravity and the environmental conditions in which they stand. Mass, translucency/opaqueness, tactility, porousness/imperviousness, acoustic properties, and so on can be included as an agreed vocabulary used in all architecture. Tectonic details, in and of themselves expressive of their composition, form a legible narrative for one building or raise a syntax across the next dozen. But how can architects reach that narrative?

Groupwork approaches each architectural project from a point of wider, deeper research without committing to an outcome of material or configuration in form until eventually it makes more sense to choose one over another. Established in 2003, Groupwork specialises in well-conceived and thoughtfully detailed new buildings, as well as restorations and refurbishments of historical buildings, applying a novel design approach to challenging and difficult sites. Throughout the past two decades of practice, a key realisation has been that the more research conducted, the greater the number of choices created, resulting in a more particular and contextually considered building. The more time that can be spent delaying a final decision means that there comes a point where it is possible to be relaxed about ideas as they crystallise and open to be a variety of choices, all of which are relevant to context.

Exploring

Broad contextual exploration can set the tone of an architectural approach, as was the case with Groupwork's project for 15 Clerkenwell Close (2017) in London – a mixed-use office and residential building with a distinctive raw limestone structural exoskeleton. The project's brief made time available for the design team to research the site's physical and historical context in order to create a solution for a building that would sit within the all-but-vanished grounds of an 11th-century limestone Norman abbey.

The investigation revealed a history of dramatic change: first an abbey building by Norman invaders; then appropriation and change of symbolism during the dissolution of the monasteries in the 16th century; Oliver Cromwell's intervention of a new and sober home; and later clearing for printing presses and rookeries made notorious by Charles Dickens and which briefly housed Karl Marx, who joined the adjacent William Morris-funded Twentieth Century Press as a contributor in the 19th century.

This storied history led to the area surrounding Clerkenwell Green becoming Islington's first conservation area in 1968. Because brick was incorrectly identified as the earliest and predominant material in the area, from the 1970s there arose a self-fulfilling prophecy of wall-to-wall new brick buildings that spanned bomb and demolition sites. These generally comprised half-brick stretcher-bond facades suspended from steel or concrete frames, nodding to their Victorian and Georgian neighbours – and thus to the area's recent past.

But this cursory historical referencing was also problematic. Houses, apartment buildings or offices often mimicked terraced row houses, which resulted in awkward floor plans and bad light levels. Had this process not been driven by commercial expediency, but allowed slower, more deliberate creative decisions, the entire Clerkenwell Green conservation area would have been better for it. Instead, the 1970s-era work diminished what it had attempted to respect and respond to, erasing its social and material authenticity. The superficiality of the resulting tone is inevitably in conflict with the area's original makers and stands as an indictment of those who encourage meaningless imitation and convention, to paraphrase Gottfried Semper and Owen Jones, the respectively German and British 19th-century architects and theorists.[1] The two connected through research assistant Jules Goury who shared their thoughts on polychrome and surface ornament as an evolution of tectonic motifs to cultural emblems.[2]

Building

Tectonics is at the core of Groupwork's work, and the project at 15 Clerkenwell Close was no exception. When exploring to gather a broader spectrum of ideas, time allows the emergence of unknown, undiscovered information able to converge otherwise conflicting areas – in short increasing the opportunities to better structure the architectural vocabulary with rhyme and reason. Had a process begun by projecting facade and form to predetermine the architectural intent, 15 Clerkenwell Close would not have evolved as it did.

Developing three loadbearing exoskeletal options, the team used structural engineering parametric software to modulate cross bracing and tapered depths of mild steel into a sparing yet stimulating three-dimensional composition. By beginning with engineering criteria, rather than a preconceived aesthetic, the possibility emerged of alluding to the intuitive half-timbered Norman structures that had once stood on the same site. In this way the project sought to step away from the superficial historical references that had characterised many of the area's projects from the late 20th century – and learn from its rich and complex architectural and material history.

Limestone had made up the formal buildings of the medieval abbey, the earliest structure on the site, and had remained common throughout London for loadbearing construction into the early 20th century. During their research, the design team reflected on why all masonry, including bricks, now typically only performs as cladding, and decided to investigate the possibility of using loadbearing masonry piers. A system was found that was low in cost, and performed better structurally and in fire safety than more Modernist systems.

It was only the Modernist preference for avoiding 'anachronistic' materials, conflating stone with the past, which had seen structural masonry jettisoned from many projects. Over a period of a hundred years, 20th-century architects had separated the structure and facade but had done so without standing back to critically rearrange the fabric of their buildings. In so doing, they unwittingly doubled both material and cost when using steel frames and adding stone cladding, increasing their carbon footprint twentyfold. These key outcomes were unknown to the Groupwork design team and suppliers prior to their research. Their choice to delay a decision to find the unforeseen is therefore one where a process of hypothesis, repeated testing and experimentation led to a new direction.

This divergence from the typical recent all-brick cladding of the Clerkenwell Green conservation area led to the controversy that surrounded the finished project. One of the most prominent examples saw an original mid-Victorian corner plot, accommodating offices above and a nightclub in its basement, replaced by new office/restaurant space on the premise that it would use costly handmade Roman bricks – which it did. The architects went to some length to lay the bricks with recessed mortar joints, horizontally as brick piers and mystifyingly as lintels too, further cutting the slender bricks down into finger-sized slips so they could be glued to precast concrete beams to appear as gravity-defying stretcher-bond brick beams.

Brick-washing elevations such as these reveals that many architects, untrained councillors and planning staff no longer understand the tectonic origins of the look that these projects attempt to imitate. In ignorance, understandably preferring the more recent fakery of the imagined past to what Groupwork acidulously sought as a fuller restoration of it in 15 Clerkenwell Close. So much so a local politician claimed a lack of clarity in the planning department's consultation procedure, starting the machinery for reversal of the project's approvals and demand for its demolition. Ultimately 15 Clerkenwell Close was saved and now stands as a victorious counterpoint to late 20th-century efforts of merely visually 'fitting in'.

Completing

Nostalgia in built form walks hand in hand with questions of style and material, and never more so than when all-but-intact structures are given special status. The higher their significance, the more pressure there is to replicate them. Yet, is this physically even possible? Are materials and techniques used in the past still available? Would their assembly meet current building regulations? Besides, what lies at the core of this desire? Are these damaged or lost buildings as singularly unique as Old Master paintings or of a level of traumatised national identity of Warsaw's town centre, for instance? Whether the latter or simply under the nebulous if not menacing guise of fitting-in, the aim and result is the idealisation of a past. Imagined and inevitably stripped of challenging social realities and physical or historical

anomalies, many restored or reconstructed buildings are, in effect, monuments, necessarily simple in narrative and consequently exclusionary and flawed.

Three Groupwork projects at 168 Upper Street (2017), Bayswater Road (2014) and Greville Street (due for completion 2021) – all in London – sit on a spectrum between 1:1 evolutions of a partially intact original language and projections of what their past architects might have completed had they the opportunity. 168 Upper Street is a terracotta-coloured concrete building that infills the end of a block, destroyed during the Second World War, with deliberately wrongly placed casting moulds. The resulting intentionally inaccurate facade allows the completed structure to subtly misremember the nostalgia of an idealised past. The concrete is cast seemingly impenetrably solid but hollow, so that when struck the building's misaligned and broken formwork reveals the inherent and permanent flaws in reconstructed monuments.

Groupwork,
168 Upper Street,
London,
2017

above: Bombed during the Second World War and vacant for 70 years, the nostalgia for past Victorian and Blitz spirit is cast as a 1:1 full loadbearing tectonic monument, with new inhabitants carving out a new life with little respect for old conventions.

below: Nostalgia is challenged through the details, which result from purposeful errors in CAD modelling, and intentionally misplaced casting moulds when pouring the 'in-situ terracotta'.

By contrast, from a distance the now-cancelled project at Bayswater Road (the council's head of planning committee thought it 'too innovative') and the ongoing project at Greville Street appear massive, solid and established. On approach, however, they are gradually revealed to be ephemeral perforated brass skins – illusions. These two projects take on Semper's extrapolation of *Kernform* and *Kunstform*, the separation of structure and decorative skin: the facade as curtain, complete with an abstracted decoration of the original tectonic joining and binding which would have been expected to sit behind. Situated adjacent to the Belle Epoque work of Mewès & Davis for the future King Edward VII and his mistress Lillie Langtry, the Bayswater Road project presents an entirely false past in its completion of an urban block facing Kensington Gardens. It reimagines its neighbour's Belle Epoque facade in woven 3mm brass, perforated to manage solar gain and privacy, glimpsed and clear views – simultaneously satisfying and criticising the desire for nostalgia.

Meanwhile, the Greville Street project resurrects eight buildings spanning onto Bleeding Heart Yard, which was described by Charles Dickens in *Little Dorrit* (1855–7) and takes its name from an inn from which Roman Catholics were taken to be martyred. The site was cleared during the 1960s for an office building and is remarkable only for presenting no street front and leaving its presence on Bleeding Heart Yard as a car park. Erected as a ghost of that past, the project reintroduces shopfronts on Greville Street. The plan also replaces the long-gone rookery on the yard with a south-facing colonnade to expand the public space while completing its deteriorated side. In this way, both projects clearly speak to their physical and historical context while reinterpreting these ideas for the future.

Groupwork,
Greville Street,
London,
due for completion 2021

opposite left: This project presents a suspended curtain on Bleeding Heart Yard with a dense solid-to-void ratio as a facsimile of the eight separate 18th- and 19th-century buildings that were cleared to make way for offices built in 1969. At a distance it appears reassuringly established, but on proximity this is revealed to be but an illusion.

opposite right: This detail shows a 1:1 fabricated demonstration panel erected onto the retained 1960s office building – it is 3mm pre-patinated brass with 60:40 solid-to-void ratio.

Groupwork,
Bayswater Road,
London,
2014

above right: The project at Bayswater Road had a Belle Epoque context on Kensington Gardens and Hyde Park. Its desire for luxury was extrapolated from the Mewès & Davis Inverness Terrace, completing the urban block to Queensway.

right: The spartan structural frame and sealed interior open to a 2-metre- (6 ½-foot-) wide winter garden, offering privacy and acoustic transition, while the suspended perforated facade functions as a brise-soleil.

Context and Craft

In *The Craftsman* (2008), sociologist Richard Sennett poses the argument that it takes 10,000 hours for an apprentice to achieve technical mastery in a field of practice, after which innovations will arise from experimentation.[3] Through the process of researching materials, focusing on context and allowing projects to coalesce into a final form, Groupwork aims to do something similar as designers. Projects such as 15 Clerkenwell Close, 168 Upper Street, Bayswater Road and Greville Street emerge from the studio's commitment to a research-based design practice that honours and embraces a plurality of styles and material technologies to suit myriad contextual cases. In this way Groupwork's approach respects the past, whether ancient or recent, rather than cursorily imitating it, creating buildings that are meaningful in both their present and future contexts. ⌂

Notes
1. See Gottfried Semper, *Style in the Technical and Tectonic Arts; Or, Practical Aesthetics* [1862], trans Harry Francis Mallgrave and Michael Robinson, Getty Publications (Los Angeles, CA), 2004, p 750, and Owen Jones, *The Grammar of Ornament*, Day & Son (London), 1856, p 67.
2. Margaret Olin, 'Self-Representation: Resemblance and Convention in Two Nineteenth-Century Theories of Architecture and the Decorative Arts', *Zeitschrift für Kunstgeschichte*, 49 (3), 1986, pp 376–97.
3. Richard Sennett, *The Craftsman*, Yale University Press (New Haven, CT and London), 2008, p.20.

Léa-Catherine Szacka

The television occupied a central place in the dining room of the house. Placed at the end of a triangular-shaped table, it allowed the audience's view to be permanently focused on the screen, even when eating.

SCREEN'S

Ugo La Pietra
with Gianfranco
Bettetini and
Aldo Grasso,
Telematic House,
61st Fiera
Internazionale
di Milano,
Milan,
1982

In the bedroom, the double bed was split in two, with each half having its separate screen so as to emphasise the increasingly individual consumption of television in the early 1980s.

The Telematic House was also a space of (auto)surveillance. Next to the bedroom, a small dressing table was installed between two pink-marble columns topped by blue-neon capitals. When looking at their reflection in the mirror, the inhabitants would also see three small monitors connected to closed-circuit cameras.

D0MESTICITY

The living room of the Telematic House included a sitting area with TV armchairs with antennae and integrated monitors, produced by the Italian furniture company Zanotta.

The ubiquity of telematics and media technologies has been highly accelerated in recent years and has changed us socially and domestically. New notions of augmented realities are being developed that suggest novel, communal yet individually decorated and populated ways to share living spaces for socialising, play and love. **Léa-Catherine Szacka**, Senior Lecturer in Architectural Studies at the University of Manchester, looks at a few examples.

FROM THE POSTMODERN

In April 1982, Italian artist, architect and designer Ugo La Pietra exhibited La Casa Telematica (Telematic House) at the 61st Fiera Internazionale di Milano, an annual fair held in the city since the early 20th century. The project explored the implications of electronic memory and the potential impact of engineering and technology on domestic spaces. Beyond its techno-utopian rhetoric, La Pietra's house characterised the shift between the radical ethos of the 1970s and the postmodern aesthetics of the 1980s: a total embrace of unbridled consumerism resulting in a house full of screens and cameras dominated by abstracted columns, neon lights and pastel colours.

Thirty-six years later, UK-based multidisciplinary design studio Space Popular, founded by Lara Lesmes and Fredrik Hellberg, exhibited The Venn Room at the 2019 Tallinn Architecture Biennale. Depicting a series of possible scenarios of cohabitation in which issues of integration, interface, exposure, overlap, representation, storage and ownership related to the use of augmented reality in the domestic environments, the project used a particularly bold aesthetic to discuss the future of our private interiors.

Despite their differences in time and location, both projects address the disruption of the traditional space of the house by media technologies, and what is more, they present some interesting aesthetic similarities. Today, Space Popular, like other young architectural practices, are exploring and reinterpreting postmodern design approaches through the practice of display, while questioning the current and future relationship between architecture and media: from television to virtual reality and social media.

The Media House

The complex relationship between domestic architecture and (social) media that we see and experience today is obviously embedded in a long history. The 'home of the future' was an obsession of the 20th century,[1] and television sets were often an integral part of these modern interiors. In 1927, Richard Buckminster Fuller's Dymaxion House, a 150-square-metre (1,600-square-foot) radically new environment for dwelling characterised by its gaining of maximum advantage from minimal energy input, was the first in a series of homes of tomorrow to include a television set.[2]

In 1956, and in the context of the 'This is Tomorrow' exhibition at the Whitechapel Art Gallery in London, artist Richard Hamilton produced the collage *Just what is it that makes today's home's so different, so appealing?*, an image that is now among the most famous in British postwar art. The collage – which is made of images sourced from popular media, in particular a stash of American magazines – points to the increasing importance and centrality of the television in 1950s British domestic life. From Alison and Peter Smithson's 1956 House of the Future, built for the Daily Mail Ideal Home Exhibition, to François Dallegret's 1965 set of drawings for Reynar Banham's article 'A Home is Not a House',[3] most modern representations of the domestic insisted on the presence of multiple screens.

These futuristic visions reveal how over the course of the 20th century, television and media in general started to dominate domestic space, bringing the outside world inside and becoming the primary vehicle for public opinion. In her 1995 article 'The

HOUSE TO **OUR** HOUSE

Media House', Beatriz Colomina commented on this intimacy of the public and the private as channelled by the media: 'The contemporary house, with its television, computer networks, fax machines, and so on, has become a much more public space than the streets of the city.'[4]

In the heyday of Postmodernism, the expansion of cable television, with the notable arrival of Ted Turner's 24-hours news-based pay-television channel Cable News Network (CNN) in June 1980 and the music video channel MTV in August 1981, modified once again the relationship between screens and domesticity. The television ceased to be the single focal point of the home and the symbol of family togetherness. Instead it transformed into a multiplicity of screens with no specific rhythm of programming, rather a constant flow of media content, privately consumed by individuals in different parts of the house.

In his book *Seeing Things: Television in the Age of Uncertainty* (1996), John Ellis defines three eras in the development of television – scarcity, availability and plenty – and explains how television performs different functions in each. From the early 1980s, in the era of availability, he suggests, scheduling became competitive as broadcasters responded to the 'narrativisation' of audience research, programming to identified differences in demographics.[5] Echoing Jean-François Lyotard's diagnosis of Postmodernism as the end of metanarratives, in the era of availability, the multiplication of screens went hand in hand with the increased targeting of content towards different members of the household.[6]

The Telematic House

The transformation of the traditional Modernist media house into forms of postmodern domesticity was also manifested stylistically. In 1972, just when colour television started to be widespread in America, outselling black-and-white units, the Museum of Modern Art (MoMA) in New York organised the now-legendary exhibition 'Italy: The New Domestic Landscape'. Curated by Emilio Ambasz, the exhibition is now seen as a milestone that contributed to the building of a new landscape linking media, design and architecture while arguably marking the moment in which the Italian radicals started to follow a more (American) commercial aesthetic. Displaying plastic-made micro-environments and objects in bright colours, it departed from the intellectual anti-consumer utopias to reveal architects and designers moving towards forms of expression that subsumed the structure of the capitalist economic cycle.[7]

It was in the context of 'Italy: The New Domestic Landscape' that Ugo La Pietra started thinking about a telematic house. Indeed, for that exhibition he had developed a series of drawings and collages in which he created an environment where telecommunication systems were used to overcome the 'barrier' that separates us from reality.[8] In this initial version, the house was symbolised by the archetype of the triangle and became 'a place of gathering, processing and dissemination of information from the public to the private realm and likewise'.[9]

Some 10 years later, when La Pietra (together with Gianfranco Bettetini and Aldo Grasso) built a full-scale version of the Telematic House for the Milan fair, the political and social context of Italy had completely changed. In the 1980s, Milan was at the centre of the so-called 'second miracle' (the first one being the economic boom of the immediate postwar period). This second period of great prosperity was based on the transformation away from heavy industry and towards a post-industrial economy centred on media, services and the creative industries. As explained by historian John M Foot in his article 'From Boomtown to Bribesville' (1999), during the 1980s Milan became the centre of fashion and design, but also publishing, advertising and commercial television.[10]

Not unlike its 1972 iteration, La Pietra's exhibition house was presented as a space where people came together and which embodied early developments in telematics and their associated new rituals. It suggested a new sensory sphere in which the information and spectacle prevails, with the home transformed into a theatre where everyone was at once actor, spectator and set designer.[11] The house itself looked like a television set in which different domestic spaces were adapted to the presence of the television screens. While the dining table mutated into a triangular shape focusing on the television set, the living room presented a multiplicity of richly decorated armchairs, each equipped with its own screen at the back. The more intimate space of the bedroom included a vanity table equipped with surveillance cameras and a control station formed by three miniature screens, and a double bed split in two, each half having its own separate screen.

In this futuristic version of the home, spaces like the dining area or the sleeping area were adapted to the invasive presence of the television screen. Yet the changes were corrective and cosmetic rather than structural. Aesthetically, the house also presented many of the common tropes of postmodern architecture: primary shapes and abstractions of the column, neon lights, fake marbles and bold colours. La Pietra's project constituted a key example of the postmodern media house in which screens multiply while media content invades the domestic space, increasingly blurring the boundaries between the simulacra of the set and the reality of the house.

The VR House

Founded in 2013 by Lara Lesmes and Fredrik Hellberg, London-based practice Space Popular are known for their use of kaleidoscopic polychromy, patterns and ornament as well as their deep interest in immersive installations and virtual reality (VR). In 2019, in the context of the Tallinn Architecture Biennale, the studio designed The Venn Room, a project that suggests a series of possible domestic cohabitations generated by the use of virtual reality in private space. In several ways, it could be read as a contemporary reinterpretation of La Pietra's 1982 project: in addition to the techno-utopian similarities between the two, The Venn Room, like many of Space Popular's projects, is reminiscent of the 1980s postmodern aesthetic.[12]

Primarily concerned with the future of virtual togetherness in the home, The Venn Room speculates on the merging of one home with the other, leading to the creation of new spaces – a series of literal Venn rooms. As Space Popular explain, 'collectively with others you will create shared environments where you hang out, play, and watch movies. You will co-decorate these environments and make them meaningful with colours, objects, and patterns that may be just built for the occasion or highly valued and kept over time.'[13] Some of the overlaps become meaningful and are decorated or highlighted with ornamental floating objects, colourful neon-like pipes running through the walls, or playful shapes emerging from the dining-room corner.

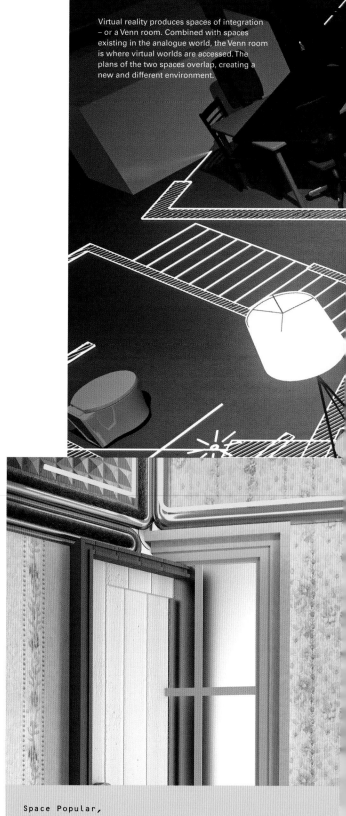

Virtual reality produces spaces of integration – or a Venn room. Combined with spaces existing in the analogue world, the Venn room is where virtual worlds are accessed. The plans of the two spaces overlap, creating a new and different environment.

Space Popular,
The Venn Room,
Tallinn Architecture Biennale,
Tallinn,
2019

Virtual reality brings together distinct homes into a shared virtual realm, therefore constructing a form of collective domestic space that frames interactions: a surprising intersection between a window and a door and different wall finish. In experiences of VR, the homes can be collectively arranged and decorated for the occasion and carry the symbols, imprints and memorabilia of their use over time.

When the physical and virtual merge, every object has the potential to be smart. Every fitting, button, handle, knob, moulding, cornice, ledge can become a switch, gate or window linking to worlds beyond that in which they materially exist. The higher the density of detail and ornamentation, the greater the opportunities for access to be granted.

For Space Popular, the introduction of virtual portals in the home – such as the television, computer or smartphone – while having considerable consequences in our day-to-day existence, has in contrast left the architecture of the home mostly untouched. With the Telematic House almost 40 years earlier, La Pietra had proposed that the media was detached from the body and the space took the aesthetic of the media itself – television and early computers. For VR there would need to be more significant transformations of the domestic space.

While Space Popular – as many other designers before them – are reticent in positing any direct association between their work and postmodern architecture, they use media and representation as a way to explain formal similarities with the bold aesthetic of the 1980s. Trying to make sense of their frequent association with Postmodernism, and denying any direct inspiration, they comment: 'The way that we think about this [is to look] from now and backward rather than from then and forward. A lot of our work deals with media, specifically media in the virtual sense of the term (virtual reality, etc). We are particularly interested in the moment in which we start to inhabit media, not being outside of it but being inside of it … And when you create a piece of media that is inhabitable, the world is pure representation, which means it's a world made of language, highly referential.'[14]

Rather than 'Postmodernism', Space Popular prefer to advocate for what they call a 'haptic revival'. As Lesmes explains: 'It's a term that other practitioners like the contemporary design studio Six N. Five are using, and that we have been testing recently as a way to explain the renewed interest in the sense of touch and the importance of materials (natural and synthetics) as a form reaction to the parametricism of the last decades.'[15]

Ubiquity

Today, media technology and our relationship to screens is drastically different from what it was in the early 1980s. If parallels are to be made between the staging of dystopian domesticity by Ugo La Pietra and the intricate spaces proposed decades later by Space Popular, stylistic similarities appear unavoidable. In their 2020 exhibition 'Freestyle: Architectural Adventures in Mass Media' at the Royal Institute of British Architects (RIBA) in London, Space Popular explored key moments in the evolution of architectural styles over the last 500 years and its relationship to the evolution of mass media. Advocating a McLuhan-esque approach, they are clear that they 'never look at the content of the media',[16] with the exhibition showing how far architectural styles reflect innovations.

While at the start of the 1980s, televisions and computers were only beginning to invade and transform our domestic environment, today the media is ubiquitous and transcendental. With the outbreak of COVID-19, domestic and private environments turned into public spaces and theatres of the everyday. Now more than ever, we live in media houses where screens are the ultimate mediators between inside and outside. The real and the simulacra get superimposed, creating an advanced level of individualism that allows us to – paradoxically – live together. One understanding of Postmodernism, it could be argued, is the aesthetic response to this fundamental shift in how we consume media. It is perhaps, therefore, precisely through this sense of ubiquity that we can connect, through style, La Pietra's Telematic House and Space Popular's Venn Room, despite the radically different technological and media landscapes they are embedded in. ∆

Notes
1. Eszter Steierhoffer, 'Introduction', *Home Futures: Living Yesterday's Tomorrow*, exh cat, Design Museum (London), 2018, p 9.
2. Lynn Spigel, *Make Room for TV: Television and the Family Ideal in Postwar America*, University of Chicago Press (Chicago, IL), 1992.
3. Reyner Banham, 'A Home is Not a House', *Art in America*, Vol 2, 1965, pp 70–9.
4. Beatriz Colomina, 'The Media House', *Assemblage*, 27, August 1995, pp 56–7.
5. John Ellis, *Seeing Things: Television in the Age of Uncertainty*, IB Tauris (London), 2000, p 82.
6. Jean-François Lyotard, *La condition postmoderne: rapport sur le savoir*, Les Éditions de Minuit (Paris), 1979. See also the exhibition 'Les Immatériaux' curated by Lyotard and presented at the Centre Pompidou, 28 March–15 July 1985.
7. See Felicity Scott, 'Architecture or Techno-Utopia', *Grey Room*, 3, Spring 2001, pp 112–26.
8. See Dpr-Barcelona: www.flickr.com/photos/77962574@N00/sets/72157626047490973/.
9. Fosco Lucarelli, 'Ugo La Pietra, La Casa Telematica, 1971', Socks, 22 November 2011: http://socks-studio.com/2011/11/22/ugo-la-pietra-la-casa-telematica/.
10. John M Foot, 'From Boomtown to Bribesville: the Images of the City, Milan, 1980–97', *Urban History*, 26 (3), December 1999, pp 393–412.
11. See the film *La Casa Telematica*: www.youtube.com/watch?v=5FCo0wdm4Lg.
12. See, for example, Olly Wainwright, 'Cheeky, Cartoonish … and Under Threat: Why Our Postmodern Buildings Must be Saved', *The Guardian*, 22 November 2017: www.theguardian.com/artanddesign/2017/nov/22/cheeky-cartoonish-under-threat-postmodern-buildings-must-be-saved.
13. See www.spacepopular.com/exhibitions/2019---the-venn-room.
14. Interview with the author, 9 April 2020.
15. *Ibid*.
16. *Ibid*.

Space Popular,
'Freestyle: Architectural Adventures in Mass Media' exhibition,
Royal Institute of British Architects (RIBA),
London,
2020

Presented online and at the RIBA, Space Popular's exhibition uses virtual reality to tackle one of the most enduring concerns of architecture: the rise and fall of architectural styles.

Owen Hopkins

TAKING JOY SERIOUSLY

AN INTERVIEW WITH ARTIST AND DESIGNER CAMILLE WALALA

Co-Guest-Editor of this edition of △D Owen Hopkins interviews artist and designer Camille Walala, exploring her work, her design process and her admiration for the 1980s Italian design group Memphis. Walala brings wild colourful exuberance to drab urban spaces and also develops invigorating, almost psychedelic interiors.

It is hard to believe that it has been just five years since Camille Walala transformed a drab office building in East London into a joyous temple of colour and pattern. Having spent several years working under the radar after graduating with a degree in textiles from Brighton University in 2009, the *Dream Come True Building* (2015) brought Walala's exuberant aesthetic to broad public view and set her on track to becoming one of London's most sought-after designers. Since then, a slew of commissions have seen her bold colours and striking patterns appear in projects all over the world.

Walala's aesthetic sensibility was shaped early on: 'My parents were a strong influence on my love of colour. I grew up in Provence, which is very colourful – the houses, the countryside and the bright blue sky. My mum had a strong sense of style. All the rooms in our house had different colours with a lot of Moroccan patterns in textiles and prints.' This environment was in stark contrast to that of Walala's father, 'an architect in Paris who was more of a minimalist; he liked strong lines. I used to go to his office and really enjoyed being in this environment, which was so simple, just grey and black and white, but with a few little pieces of colour.'

Another early influence was the artist Sonia Delaunay, a key figure in the Parisian avant-garde, both for her strongly graphic abstraction and for the way she mixed disciplines and media: 'She was one of the first to push art in scenography, objects, textiles, clothes, into everyday life. She even designed a pavilion for the 1925 international exhibition in Paris.' For Walala, Delaunay remains a constant touchstone: 'Seeing her work was the first time I realised I could mix things.'

Camille Walala, *Walala x Industry City*, Sunset Park, Brooklyn, New York, 2018

previous page: To create this mural for the annual NYCxDESIGN festival, Walala developed a 3D-effect design that accentuated the architectural features of the building. Working with a team of decorative painters from Industry City-based landmark-building specialists EverGreene Architectural Arts, the transformation took 12 days.

Camille Walala, *Dream Come True Building*, Shoreditch, London, 2015

right: Invited by the building's occupants, the post-production studio Splice, to introduce colour and character to the exterior, Walala worked with a team of eight volunteers recruited via Instagram who spent 10 days transforming the five-storey building into a kinetic melange of colours, stripes and zigzags.

And, of course, there is the Memphis Group, founded in
Milan in 1981 by Ettore Sottsass: 'I first remember finding
these books on Memphis designs shortly after graduating; it
was a moment of hysterical joy. They encapsulated so much
of what I love about design and art.' Although Memphis was
relatively short-lived and commercially not very successful,
its influence was huge, in many ways defining the look of the
1980s. For Walala, 'having grown up in the 1980s myself,
there was nostalgia, too'. This is perhaps why it is not simply
the Memphis aesthetic we see in her work, but its almost
childlike sense of freedom and fearless spirit. 'I'm always
drawn to the kids' section in bookshops', she adds.

Other influences range from Mexican Modernists Luis
Barragán and Ricardo Legorreta ('I've just come back from
Mexico,' Walala reports), to the New York Pop artist Keith
Haring ('There is a warm personality in his work') and the
enigmatic Bolivian architect Freddy Mamani ('His brain is
just exploding with pattern'). And it is not hard to see echoes
of all of these in Walala's work, both stylistically and in
terms of informing her ethos and approach. As she says, they
are 'all the pieces of a puzzle. It felt like a natural continuity
to use colour in my work.'

WORKING PRACTICES

Despite her success and the confidence her work exudes,
Walala says she still occasionally suffers from 'imposter
syndrome': 'I can't draw,' she readily admits, 'I find it hard
to use design programmes. I can't really sketch.' Instead her
process relies on a kind of constant creative nourishment,
almost of design as a way of life: 'Every morning I try to
make something – a collage, or even some mark-making.
Everything is usually very flat when I work with it. I often
go back to something I've created this way when I've got a
project. I like to play, to be creative with no reason. But it's
much harder to work when under pressure.'

Collaboration has long been part of Walala's practice,
working closely with her creative producer Julia Jomaa and
a range of other freelancers, depending on the nature of each
project and the particular expertise required. 'It's a playful
method,' Walala notes, 'constantly back and forth.' These
collaborations extend to architecture: 'I love the challenge
of an architectural project. I like working with a restriction.
A blank piece of paper is too hard.' However, for her
architectural projects those restrictions are not simply of site
or budget, but of working with an existing building, though
this is one she happily embraces: 'the uglier the better'.

Camille Walala,
Walala Lounge,
South Molton Street,
London,
2019

Describing her motivations for the project, Walala notes how 'I wanted to push myself by creating public art in another style, to make people smile again, but this time with public benches, where people could feel at home, surrounded by plants and rugs.'

This was the case for her breakthrough project, the *Dream Come True Building,* and also for her best-known project to date, the much-photographed *Walala x Industry City* (2018) in Brooklyn, New York. While the latter was not exactly an ugly building, it was a dull one. 'It was very repetitive,' Walala recalls, 'and I wanted to give it another life, to make it become 3D. The site is bathed in the most beautiful colours at sunset, which has inspired my palette for the project.' She made two designs: one, a single composition based around a large shape, and the other the design that was ultimately realised. On paper the first one looked more impressive, but Walala impressed upon the client that the second would work better at the much bigger scale of the building: 'They trusted me which was really nice.'

Generally, Walala has been lucky with her clients, something that success makes easier: 'I'm trying to work with people who I really like. I always want to follow my gut. I'm not good at compromising. If it's a question of budget that's one thing, but if it's about taste that's different. I used to accept the client's view. But I've realised that if they've chosen me for a project, they like my work, so they will have to trust me.'

It is rare for a designer or artist to get the opportunity to work at the scale of architecture. If they do, it is usually in a way that is complementary to yet distinct from an architectural project. There is the architecture and then there is the art. But *Industry City* is a fusion of the two: an artistic intervention into architecture. Although physically that intervention is only as deep as a lick of paint – what an architect might dismiss as nothing more than surface – its effect has been transformational, both socially and culturally.

This is a paradox that many architects and even designers are still wary of, but not the Postmodernists. Instructive here is a comment by Sottsass's friend and fellow designer Alessandro Mendini, who maintained perhaps counterintuitively that 'superficiality has depth if understood and accepted as the profound difficulty of human life'.[1] This was one of Postmodernism's key lessons: rejecting the Modernist notion that a rational proposition automatically requires a rational-looking building – rectilinear and rejecting ornament – and instead embracing the cultural possibilities of surface and style. Memphis was in many ways the embodiment of this ethos.

But Walala takes it a step further. Asked to sum up her work, she says it is about 'taking joy seriously'. 'Joy is underrated,' she continues; 'I love the idea of bringing an element of fun to the street, weaving colour and joy into a city which is sometimes lacking in both.' It is a wonderfully refreshing viewpoint. Few designers or architects discuss joy in such an open and engaging way, tending to be rather more interested in the means (the project itself) than its effect – how it might make us feel. In this view, joy is at best a byproduct of a successful project. For Walala, it is the whole point, with her signature bright colours and bold patterns the way she goes about realising this understated yet radical mission.

COLOUR IN CONTEXT

The best designs are often those the client does not realise they need until they see them. So it was with Walala's project for South Molton Street in Mayfair, London. Initially, Walala recalls, the client, Grosvenor, was thinking of a mural or a zebra crossing, like those she designed for Better Bankside Business Improvement District in Southwark. 'But when we went to the site we realised there was nowhere to sit, so we decided to create some benches … where people can gather, appreciate their surroundings and enjoy the city.' This became *Walala Lounge* – offering both places to sit and talk and bringing a bit of unexpected colour and joy to a smart Mayfair street. 'Someone said, "I smile every time I pass them." For me, that's the best compliment.'

When conceiving a project, Walala is highly aware of the setting in which her work will sit, and also the expectations people have of it. This was never truer than for her project *Villa Walala* at Broadgate in the City of London in 2017. 'It's really smart and corporate, so I decided to do something unexpected: a massive inflatable. I wanted to bring that element of surprise, to make people react, to think what the hell is this inflatable in this financial district?' While deeply 'playful' (a word Walala is happy to embrace as a description of her work), the project succeeded in putting Broadgate on the map for a different demographic: 'No one usually goes there at the weekend. But it was full of people, and lots of families. It was bringing the city back to the people.'

Camille Walala,
Villa Walala,
London Design Festival,
London,
2017

For the festival's 15th anniversary, Walala was selected by festival partner British Land to create the landmark project. *Villa Walala* was what she came up with. Made from blocks of vinyl adorned with digitally printed patterns, the villa's vibrant tones, tactile surfaces and engaging shapes provided a striking contrast to its monochrome surroundings.

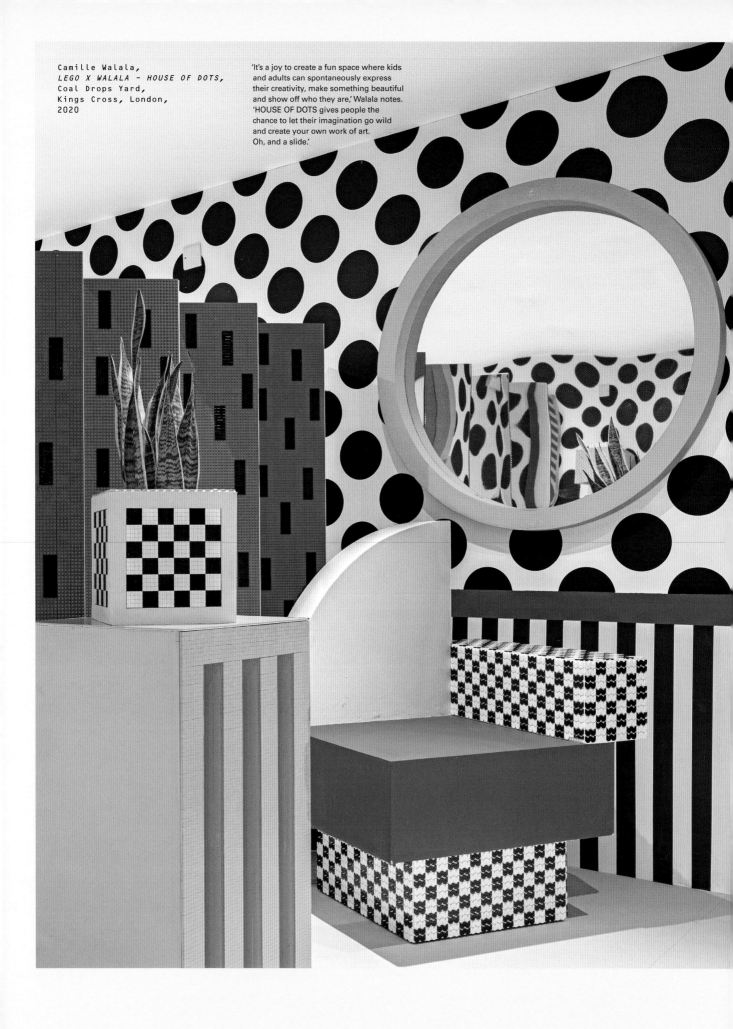

Camille Walala,
LEGO X WALALA - HOUSE OF DOTS,
Coal Drops Yard,
Kings Cross, London,
2020

'It's a joy to create a fun space where kids and adults can spontaneously express their creativity, make something beautiful and show off who they are,' Walala notes. 'HOUSE OF DOTS gives people the chance to let their imagination go wild and create your own work of art. Oh, and a slide.'

If British Land commissioned Walala at Broadgate because her work was the opposite of their traditional corporate image, LEGO approached her because it was a perfect fit aesthetically and in ethos: 'I say no to a lot of brand work when it's commercial. But LEGO – that was a perfect match. They said do whatever you want, so I did a two-storey house.' The project was to mark the launch of LEGO Dots – two-dimensional tiles that come in different shapes and colours that can be combined to make various patterns on surfaces. *HOUSE OF DOTS* (2020), as Walala christened the project, used over two million pieces to create a number of rooms each with its own distinct character. The result was, in Walala's eyes, the 'perfect kids' dream house'.

As well as being a big hit with those who experience them in person, Walala's projects have enjoyed huge popularity on Instagram, where she is at the forefront of a number of designers who are embracing colour and pattern. While acknowledging social media's upsides, she remains cautious of some of its unintended consequences: 'On social media the tendency is for everything to look the same, so I try not to look at it too much. I want to be sure that I'm doing something because I like it, not because I saw something on social media.'

In this she identifies a sometimes-overlooked aspect of social media culture. It is common now for critics to hit out at architects who appear to be consciously designing for Instagram likes, but in practice the unconscious influence of social media likely has a far greater impact. For Walala, what matters is remaining true to herself and her principles, while applying her patterns 'to different media and different settings'.

Talking to Walala, it is hard not to be struck by the passion that runs through her work, and her sincere desire to bring joy to the people who experience it. But that is not to say she thinks everything should be brightly coloured and boldly patterned: 'When I work, I am really aware of whatever is around. Colour can be beautiful, but really clashing. *The Dream Come True Building* on Old Street looks better in a grey setting.'

One way of understanding Walala's work, therefore, is as the striking exception to the perhaps necessary mundaneness of the everyday. Like her hero Sottsass, her projects are full of emotion and personality, having an almost spiritual presence. They revel in freedom and rebellion, breaking the rules, wanting to get noticed and arguing for colour and pattern as a vital part of everyday life. 'I'm not doing my work for designers, but for people. And I'm doing it for a reason – I want to bring people together, to create spaces where people meet, hopefully with a smile on their face.' ⌂

Note
1. From the 'Design Interviews' series (2008) directed by Anna Pitscheider and co-edited by Museo Alessi and Corraini Edizioni. Quoted in Glenn Adamson and Jane Pavitt (eds), *Postmodernism: Style and Subversion, 1970–1990*, V&A Publishing (London), 2011, p 88.

Camille Walala,
End Youth Homelessness,
London,
2019

For this project, Walala joined forces with the multi-charity initiative End Youth Homelessness on a nationwide campaign to raise awareness of its Employability Fund. Walala's design was inspired by the idea of the maze and the simple, powerful message that 'Education is the route from homeless to home'.

Perceiving Postmodernism

David Kohn

Learning from London's Marshlands

David Kohn,
Thames river wall
at Thurrock,
Essex,
1996

In 1996 Kohn photographed the
lower Thames corridor, from
Barking to Tilbury and from
Woolwich to Gravesend, taking
photographs of the varied
landscapes. This was a generous
urbanism that welcomed
all-comers and suggested an
unassuming model for other
places.

David Kohn Architects
and Fiona Banner,
A Room for London,
Queen Elizabeth Hall,
London,
2012

The view from A Room for London
stretches from the Houses of
Parliament in the west to St Paul's
Cathedral in the east. In the centre
of this panorama is the Savoy
Hotel (1899) which opened the
same year as Joseph Conrad's
novella *Heart of Darkness* was
published. It was the first luxury
hotel of its kind in Britain and
designed to attract international
visitors to the capital.

David Kohn, director of London-based David Kohn Architects and diploma tutor at the Architectural Association, takes us on an almost psychogeographic dérive along the River Thames and into its marshy hinterland, picking up nuances, his own buildings and high points of the postmodern past. Along the way he explains what is important and inspiring for him and his practice.

Can it really be true that not all views are equal? And if this is the case, is it possible, or desirable, to make the narrative embedded in the view of London that is spread out before me available to everybody in Britain?

— Caryl Phillips, 'A Bend in the River', 2013[1]

Learning from the existing landscape is a way of being revolutionary for an architect.

— Robert Venturi, Denise Scott Brown and Steven Izenour, *Learning from Las Vegas*, 1972[2]

Across the River Thames from Canary Wharf, beside London's O2 Arena, a small, light industrial building designed by David Kohn Architects is under construction. It is one of 16 buildings aiming to provide affordable workspace for creative businesses on the Greenwich Peninsula, a kind of modern-day guild-house quarter. An oversized illuminated sign on its roof announces your arrival at the Design District. At the building's base is a squat red colonnade that seems scaled more to the whole district than to the building itself. Between the sign and the colonnade is a grid of green aluminium frames that make it difficult to read how many storeys the building contains. On its front corners stand two 4-metre- (13-foot-) tall figures with outstretched arms.

This building references many sources: from Robert Venturi, Denise Scott Brown and Steven Izenour's 1972 ode to signs, *Learning from Las Vegas*, to the use of statuary in the facades of craft guilds of Venice and Antwerp, to James Stirling's 1984 Stuttgart Neue Staatsgalerie and his 1988 conversion of the mid-19th-century Albert Dock into Tate Liverpool. Despite appearances, it was not the intention to either make a 'postmodern' building or to reference this style, which was popularised during the 1960s–70s and achieved notoriety in the 1980s–90s. So why the quotation, the ornament, the ambiguity? Why the indeterminacy, the signs, the sculpture, the colour – and crucially, why now?

To address these questions, this article traces a journey from the centre of London to the marshlands in the east of the city and beyond. En route landmarks, landscapes and previous work by DKA are discussed in order to shed light on those aspects of Postmodernism that are meaningful to the practice's design approach and how this is relevant to contemporary architectural discourse in the widest sense.

David Kohn Architects,
Design District, Greenwich, London,
due for completion 2021

opposite: The building makes references to the work of Robert Venturi and Denise Scott Brown, James Stirling, Pierre Chareau and the guild houses of Venice.

right: Being on a peninsula that projects into the Thames, the Design District appears close to Canary Wharf, even though there is a gulf between them.

Thanks for the Blinds

An important earlier DKA project that has informed the practice's approach at the Greenwich Design District was A Room for London. The brief was to create a venue on the roof of the Queen Elizabeth Hall for the duration of the 2012 Cultural Olympiad that would allow visitors to contemplate the capital. Designed in collaboration with the artist Fiona Banner, the Room liberally employed quotation and narrative as design tools in the hope of creating a context in which London's contemporary cultural and political issues might be addressed. The design was inspired by Joseph Conrad's *Heart of Darkness*,[3] a novella written in 1899 that begins with a sailor, Charles Marlow, on the deck of a ship moored on the banks of the Thames, recounting a journey he made to the Congo to find a shadowy figure named Kurtz. The story is a terrifying dissection of the mindset of empire, revealing the depths to which Kurtz has descended in his treatment of the local population, and was written three years after the International Olympics Committee hosted the first modern Olympics in Athens – a project of empires to which most non-European nations were not invited.

The Room liberally employed quotation and narrative as design tools in the hope of creating a context in which London's contemporary cultural and political issues might be addressed

David Kohn Architects and Fiona Banner, A Room for London, Queen Elizabeth Hall, London, 2012

The one-room installation, perched high above the South Bank, was inspired by Joseph Conrad's novella *Heart of Darkness* (1899).

The design took the form of a boat-like pavilion, named the *Roi des Belges* after the paddle steamer Conrad had himself piloted up the Congo. Banner and DKA recognised that a vehicle able to connect contemporary London to its colonial past would encourage discussion about this relationship and its ongoing impact on Britain and the world. The form of the boat was built from fragments of Conrad's text and quotations from London landmarks, such as a riveted hull recalling Marlow's repairs to his steamboat and the rooftop steeple referencing Nicholas Hawksmoor's Christ Church, Spitalfields (1729). The hull was cantilevered over the edge of the Brutalist Queen Elizabeth Hall and offered a truly staggering view, from the Houses of Parliament in the west to St Paul's Cathedral in the east. The co-commissioner, Artangel, invited 13 writers-in-residence to stay aboard during the year. The novelist Caryl Phillips joined in April and wrote about the state of Britain in 2012. Phillips touched on issues ranging from identity and racism and the 7/7 bombings, to parliamentary reform and the roles of the monarchy and church in a modern state, and ideas of belonging through the literature of 1950s migrants from the West Indies. He also discussed the architecture of the iconic buildings along the north bank of the Thames which he saw as emblematic of 'exclusivity; privilege; power'.[4] Phillips did not want to 'dismiss the evidence of grandeur, achievement and tradition suggested by this landscape'[5] but was nevertheless compelled to ask how this view of central London might reflect 'the narrative of a twenty-first-century, multicultural, multiracial people'?[6] He concluded, 'Not for the first time I'm glad that Mr Conrad's boat has come equipped with window blinds'.[7]

Later, Phillips decided to take a trip downstream on a Thames Clipper in search of 'other visions of London'. Along the way he called out various landmarks he encountered – from the Tower of London to Canary Wharf and the O2 Arena – which he variously described as an 'astonishing array',[8] 'mirage'[9] and 'extraterrestrial'.[10] On his 'return to my own little rooftop boat',[11] Phillips reflected how he had 'found many Londons which … made me feel slightly more comfortable with my iconically powerful view'.[12] He wondered how the city might learn from its periphery, which is 'no less representative' of London but which ultimately offers no substitute for the role the centre of London performs as symbolic of British culture.

A Monumental Joke

Marking the boundary between the city proper and its eastern hinterland, One Canada Square is the tallest and most distinctive building in Canary Wharf – described by Phillips as a 'Dubai-like spectacle'.[13] Designed by Cesar Pelli, when completed in 1991 it was also the tallest tower in the country. Its 50 storeys topped with a pyramid and flashing light to ward off planes approaching City Airport, the building is arguably the type of Postmodernism that architects loved to hate: brash, shiny, superficial, seemingly hollowed-out. That the style was used for a boosterist regeneration

project that dramatically failed with the 1993 collapse of the owners, Canadian property giant Olympia & York, added Schadenfreude to the general air of disapproval.

Projects like One Canada Square were one of the final nails in Postmodernism's coffin, even though at the same time Venturi Scott Brown's complex alternative vision of Postmodernism was taking centre stage next door to the National Gallery. It was perhaps the lack of complexity in the form of One Canada Square that made it a monumental joke of the kind that seeks to assert superiority. In so doing, Postmodernism's goliath pitted itself against Modernism's own corporate variety, in an unedifying fight to the death. But in truth Canary Wharf, like the banks after it, was too big to fail and nowadays is grudgingly accepted as having succeeded on its own terms, even if the original ambition to create such a monocultural second financial hub for London remains tragically misguided.

Louis Hellman,
Marketecture,
Architect's Journal,
6 April 1988

One Canada Square (1991), the centrepiece of Canary Wharf, was the largest and most conspicuous postmodern building of its day. As such it was the brunt of jokes about the superficial transformation of corporate Modernism into something that might appeal more to traditionalists.

Phillips concludes his journey a little further downstream: 'And beyond this? Well, less development and a reminder of an earlier, unregenerated Thames.' Sixteen years before Phillips's trip in the summer of 1996, I had made a similar voyage of discovery, working my way around the lower Thames corridor with a camera and methodically recording the landscapes I found. I was looking for incongruous moments where an allotment garden was beside a power station, or garden furniture laid out for tea in front of a car breaker's yard. I found that places like Rainham and Grays on the river's Essex banks had a time all of their own that stood in stark contrast to central London. Beehives hummed while mudflats wheezed as tankers crept along the horizon and Ford cars rolled off the production line.

The East Thames Corridor has, in some places, a dream-like quality where the fragments of urbanity that one knows from wildly different moments in the past now appear in new and unexpected configurations. Some situations would make you want to laugh out loud, not in disdain, but in solidarity with the breath-taking unexpectedness and originality of situations which are nonetheless, in their circumstances, completely ordinary. Such encounters upset expectations, as established in the polite centres of conurbations and architectural education where every use has its correct place and a hierarchy is unquestioningly perpetuated. If London could dream, downriver places would represent a fulfilment of all its repressed wishes.

Back to the Future

If the singular vision of One Canada Square represents one ending of Postmodernism, might the marshlands of the East Thames Corridor connect to the doctrine's more complex, earlier incarnations? Looking at Denise Scott Brown's early work, one of her chief interests is in landscape's inherent capacity to sustain heterogeneity. In recent years, Scott Brown has exhibited photographs she took on her travels and as part of her research and activism before she met her future husband and collaborator Robert Venturi. These cover the townships around Johannesburg, the city where she spent her childhood, American road trips and neighbourhoods of Philadelphia where she supported a local initiative to replan the predominantly African-American suburb to avoid destruction by a new motorway.

Scott Brown's photographs have a consistent sensibility that foregrounds the accidental in landscapes, such as signs, fragments of vernacular architecture and casual street life. In a 2013 interview she recounts how a childhood teacher left a deep impression on her by asking, 'How can you be creative if you ignore what's around you?'[14] She discusses the racial segregation in 1940s South Africa and how this made her all the more determined to document the stark differences she witnessed in Johannesburg. She acknowledges, 'My country was very bad, and I still love it for what it is and what it can be.'[15] This interest in the reality of everyday situations eventually led to *Learning from Las Vegas*, her seminal collaboration with Venturi and Izenour that brought the strip into mainstream architectural discourse. Many of the same qualities that Scott Brown sought out in landscapes during her early travels can still be found in the Lower Thames Valley with the potential to inspire new ideas about places.

Against Hubris

The issues that Caryl Phillips raised whilst staying aboard the *Roi des Belges* are no less pressing today than in 2012. The Windrush scandal, Brexit and the disproportionate impact the Coronavirus pandemic is having on BAME and poorer communities tell a story of

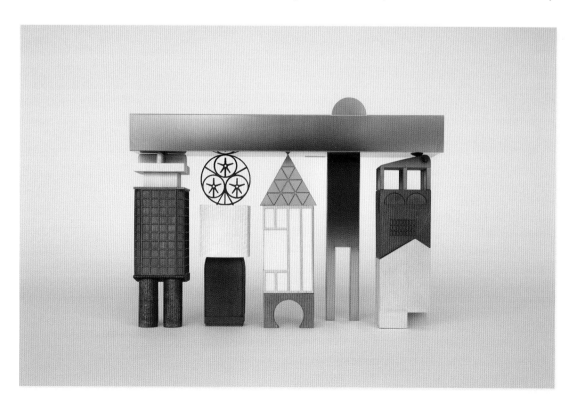

David Kohn Architects, *Five Figures for a Masque*, 2019

Model made for the exhibition 'Alternative Histories' curated by Marius Grootveld and Jantje Engels at 6 Cork Street temporary gallery, Mayfair, London. Inspired by John Hejduk's *Aerial View of Wall House* (1972), the model recombines fragments of DKA's projects to make five architectonic figures.

Denise Scott Brown,
Philadelphia,
1961

Denise Scott Brown was an avid photographer and used the results to illustrate her research and teaching. Her photography of everday urban life in Philadelphia anticipated her research into the Las Vegas Strip which she carried out with Robert Venturi and Steven Izenour.

If London could dream, downriver places would represent a fulfilment of all its repressed wishes

continued inequalities and pose difficult questions over national identity. Phillips's recognition that architecture has a part to play in allowing all Londoners the possibility of identifying with their city remains pressing. A Room for London provided a lens through which to see London with a certain clarity. Phillips's subsequent journey downriver revealed that other Londons are not so exclusive and that, within this heterogeneity, there is the hope of other forms of architecture and citymaking.

Looking directly across the river to the Savoy Hotel, it was not the building's Art Deco style that irked Phillips but its 'unselfreflective confidence'.[16] Denise Scott Brown held a similar view, although presented in its opposite form: 'I love monumental buildings that laugh at themselves a little.'[17] While coming from very different perspectives, both Phillips and Scott Brown are not preoccupied by style, but rather allowing buildings to acknowledge the limits of their ideological underpinnings. This is both a design question but also one of patronage and asking those in power to moderate any drive to monumentalise, thus avoiding the hubris that results. In periods of national and institutional doubt, the very possibility of grand gestures achieving any kind of popular recognition tips from hubris to madness and numbs those parts of architecture once able to reach any audience.

No building can address issues as complex as race and identity in contemporary Britain. However, architecture's twin potential to combine many different cultural references in a synthetic whole, as well as sustaining multiple interpretations by different users, is nonetheless a cause for optimism. Alongside better representation of minorities within the building professions and a willingness to engage with a wider set of precedents, not only architectural but from all creative disciplines and from the immediate changing world around us, there are routes to richer, more complex and more nourishing contexts that reflect the complexities of contemporary society. ⌂

Notes
1. Caryl Phillips, 'A Bend in the River', in *A London Address*, Granta (London), 2013, p 45.
2. Robert Venturi, Denise Scott Brown and Steven Izenour, *Learning from Las Vegas*, The MIT Press (Boston, MA), 1972, p 3.
3. Joseph Conrad, *Heart of Darkness*, Penguin Classics (London), 2007 (first published as a serial in 1899, and as a book in 1902).
4. Phillips, *op cit*, p 43.
5. *Ibid*, p 41.
6. *Ibid*, p 41.
7. *Ibid*, p 45.
8. *Ibid*, 44.
9. *Ibid*.
10. *Ibid*, p 45.
11. *Ibid*.
12. *Ibid*, p 44.
13. *Ibid*.
14. 'Denise Scott Brown: An African Perspective – Interviewed by Jochen Becker', *metroZones*, 2013: https://vimeo.com/312749292.
15. *Ibid*.
16. Phillips, *op cit*, p 44.
17. Andres Ramirez, 'Beside the Point: The Architectures of Denise Scott Brown', in Lukas Feireiss (ed), *Legacy: Generations of Creatives in Dialogue*, Frame Publishers (Amsterdam), 2018, pp 162–9.

**David Knight and
Cristina Monteiro**

DK-CM,
Bruce Grove
Public Conveniences,
Haringey,
London,
due for completion 2021

DK-CM are currently developing
proposals to restore and reactivate
the disused Bruce Grove Public
Conveniences in Tottenham. This
involves finding a new use for
the building which respects its
heritage whilst also providing a new,
community-focused programme to
the High Road.

WORKING IN PUBLIC

Political and Design Inheritances in the Work of DK-CM

London-based DK-CM is an architecture and urbanism practice that operates in the public sector. It is inspired by the complex heterogeneous nature of public space and its diverse personal histories, some oral, some institutional. **David Knight and Cristina Monteiro** describe their approach to community collaboration, inclusivity and designing with and for the public in all its magnificent spectrum.

We are children of the 1980s. Though originating from very different places – northern Portugal and southern England – with very different relationships to modernity, we both grew up at a time when the certainties of the 'postwar consensus' had disappeared and the world around us was absolutely 'postmodern' in the term's wider meaning: fractured, complex, multivalent, contradictory. Bits of history bobbing up and floating around us.

The education in architectural history that we then gained – together – reflected that context. In the wake of modernity and Modernism we had arrived into an era of multiple different shades of practice, all apparently acceptable and existing sometimes in different worlds. By the time we formed DK-CM in 2012, contemporary architecture could be a myriad of different things, depending on which school you went to, which magazine or journal you picked up.

We share our lives and our studio with a black-and-white spaniel called Morris, who appears to be untroubled by the powerful contradictions that shaped the life of his namesake, the 19th-century designer and social activist, William Morris: a struggle to maintain parallel commitments to aesthetics and to political activism. Our dog's day-to-day life is not defined by the agonising tension between wanting to tear down society and build it anew along just and democratic lines, and wanting to design wallpaper. We engage in those tensions for him while he looks on from his basket. We are trying to make a practice that engages head-on with architectural and spatial design for its own sake, as something important in those terms, whilst also delivering upon what we feel are our political and social responsibilities. For us, the political questions that frame a space – its potential to suggest or support new ways of living, new forms of conviviality, to enrich lives – are not reasons to ignore or suppress conversations about style, language and character, but reasons to celebrate those things and bring them to bear in that context.

Public Values

DK-CM builds and proposes in public, for the public and often with the public, and the public sector is our client. We came together out of a shared commitment to architecture's political and social role, not as the solution to anything really but as a participant in how we talk about and make our world anew. And arguing about wallpaper at the same time. So inevitably a first point of reference is the architecture of the welfare state and of the postwar period, where (amongst many other things) architecture and urban design had a powerful transformative impact on the world, often with a powerful social conscience and bulwarked by a confidence that is now hard to imagine.

Many of the results of that period are gorgeous, powerful gestures that remain valid today, whether as ideas, memories or built form. Many others – extant and not – were the cause of colossal destruction and trauma. These and everything in between were born out of a professionalism that was ambitious, powerful

DK-CM,
Erith Lighthouse,
Erith, London,
2017

Erith Lighthouse was a pavilion on the River
Thames at Erith, designed to host a series
of events throughout summer 2017. With a
structure made of theatrical rigging clad in
coloured polycarbonate, the building celebrates
the connection to the river as well as Erith's
industrial present and recent history.

and cultured but also very often characterised by an arrogance and dismissiveness to the people its projects were for, as can be found in countless examples globally, from the expressways driven through New York by Robert Moses through to the chief planner of Newcastle describing in public the residents of a redevelopment area as 'almost a separate race of people … most people who live in slums have no views on their environment at all'.[1]

The professions of architecture and planning, it seems in retrospect, had discovered the relevance of the public's actual voice just as their power to transform that voice into profound spatial change eroded away to almost nothing. In the UK, 'participation' was written into the town and country planning rulebook one year after the infamous partial collapse of the Ronan Point tower block in East London in 1968, and in the midst of ongoing popular outrage at the proposed demolition and comprehensive redevelopment of Covent Garden in central London. Meanwhile, in the US, the students of Denise Scott Brown, Robert Venturi and Steven Izenour were systematically taking apart Las Vegas in their landmark quest to understand *how and why a place was* in advance of proposing how to change it.[2]

When we look back at the last time there was a strong public sector effecting real social change, we must do so through a lens which also shows us the limitations and failures of that period. However much we long for that capacity, it is always tempered by a reading of what was too often missed out. And our commitment to an architecture that generates – or at least participates in the creation of – public value is always inflected accordingly.

Inheritances

In looking back, we also witness the extraordinary social movements and projects that emerged as the postwar consensus ended, particularly those concerned with shining new light on the actual mechanics of popular culture, working-class life and social change. We might think of Raphael Samuel, whose History Workshop (founded 1976) aimed to reconfigure historical research and writing towards the perspectives of the marginalised and disadvantaged which he dubbed 'history from below'. We might think of oral historian Tony Parker, who spent 18 months on a South London housing estate in the early 1980s interviewing and giving voice to its diverse residents, finding none of them typical, in a list that included local squatters, prefab residents and caretakers.[3] Or of QueenSpark Books, a publisher of local history and working-class autobiography that grew out of opposition to a redevelopment project in the Queens Park area of Brighton, and which continues to publish works and run diary-writing workshops in the town. Or of historian and novelist Mary Chamberlain, whose work *Fenwomen* (1975) was a then-unprecedented exploration of the desires and lives of women living and working in a remote part of the Cambridgeshire Fens.[4] Or of teacher and oral historian George Ewart Evans, sociologist Herbert Gans, and urbanist Philippe Boudon.

Then we naturally look at the architects whose work appears obviously to have been inflected by this new wave of understanding: Ralph Erskine, the Matrix Feminist Design Co-operative, Walter Segal, Venturi Scott Brown, and Giancarlo de Carlo. And the groups of architects, among them future superstars Álvaro Siza and Eduardo Souto de Moura, who worked to deliver inner-city housing for the urban poor in the immediate wake of the Portuguese revolution in 1974, in what is possibly modern architecture's most profound and tumultuous engagement with popular desire.

So we want the public commitment of the postwar period, but transformed by the shifts in understanding that came in its wake which make the simplicity and clarity of its project seem naive. No wonder the architecture we are drawn to is provisional, well put together but also clearly 'made', asymmetrical, difficult, speaking multiple languages at once. It is these attributes that draw us to some buildings and projects of the postmodern period, but they also draw us back to what we call the 'uncertain' period of Modernism when the style was not yet a style and everything was in a powerful, energising state of flux: the clad works of Hendrik Petrus Berlage, such as Holland House in London (1916); the radical conservationism of Morris and his 'Ruskinian' allies, such as the Red House, Bexleyheath (1860, designed by Philip Webb), which struggled to look forward and backward at once; Martti Välikangas's 'folk classicism' at Puu-Käpylä garden suburb in Helsinki (1925); and Gunnar Asplund hovering deliciously between Nordic classicism and modernity, most famously in the Stockholm Public Library (1928).

Thus, in making a practice we are aiming, in a hand-to-mouth sort of way, for a position that straddles the worlds set out above whilst also embracing the Morrisian tradition of juggling aesthetic and political concerns, to ultimately consider them as one practice. Except that the nature-worship that characterised the work of Morris, John Ruskin, radical poet and philosopher Edward Carpenter and so many others of the late 19th century and in that tradition must now be updated to reflect the fundamental importance of environmental issues and of rebalancing humanity's relationship to nature.

We are interested in an architecture that is an active participant in the actions, movements and conversations that form society. We want to make places and buildings that can be explored in high and low terms, that impact upon people's lives and shift possibilities and perceptions.

On special days the loggia provides a rhythm and form to market stalls, and a focal point for events. On ordinary days it is a place where kids watch other kids kick a ball on the way home from school, and where locals seek shade or shelter

DK-CM,
Barkingside Town Square,
Redbridge, London,
2015

This project reworks the underused spaces around Barkingside's great 1960s civic architecture to create meaningful, inhabitable public space. The space now hosts musical performances, theatre and promotional events, and DK-CM are now working with the borough to develop a market for the venue.

Public Projects

DK-CM's Barkingside Town Square in the London Borough of Redbridge, completed in 2015, transformed a series of public spaces around a sequence of Modernist civic buildings by Frederick Gibberd. Gibberd's work at Barkingside was brilliantly civic and generous as a series of interiors, and in the form of the lofty 'crown' of clerestory windows that are its most significant public gesture. But, reflecting his rejection of the suburb of the speculator, the spaces around the buildings – and between them and the 1920s High Street – were hard to occupy and framed by blank walls. Presented with the task of enriching that High Street, our project aimed at retrofitting Gibberd's civic Modernism with a new attitude to public space that was generous, gregarious and encouraging of both formal and informal use.

The most prominent gesture was a new loggia that reworked a blank concrete wall facing the High Street as a place for shade, shelter and inhabitation. On special days the loggia provides a rhythm and form to market stalls, and a focal point for events. On ordinary days it is a place where kids watch other kids kick a ball on the way home from school, and where locals seek shade or shelter. We once had a memorable conversation with the receptionist at the front desk who was apparently in the midst of an ongoing argument with her sister about whether the new loggia was Art Deco or not. She insisted that it was, because of the jazzy black-and-white terrazzo below the arches, but her sister was adamant that it couldn't be because it was newly built. This conversation has stayed with us because it was so good to know that an intervention of ours was causing discussions – heated ones – about the aesthetics of architecture and urban design.

The theme of conversation is a recurring one. Whether through architectural design – for example, in DK-CM's projects for Bruce Grove Public Conveniences in Haringey, North East London (due for completion 2021), Romford Market House in East London (begun 2016) and Wroughton Academy in Gorleston, Great Yarmouth, Norfolk (completed 2018) – or through the public discussions that shape a masterplan or piece of spatial policy, such as the research undertaken in Harrow, North West London, in 2018, we go in search of two-way conversations. In this way we do not abscond from questions of architectural character or style but attempt to ask those questions in public, whether as the context of a project or the project itself. For 'New Publics', our exhibition at the British School at Rome in 2019, DK-CM undertook video-conference interviews with members of the public who had experienced the English planning system first hand, where we drew out their experiences and propositions for planning and placed them together in the gallery, unmediated. The project built upon 'Making Planning Popular', David's doctoral research at the Royal College of Art (2018) which remarkably was the first attempt to research public perception of the UK planning system since 1995 and the first to do so with particular attention to the shifts in knowledge-exchange and communication that have happened since the arrival of the ubiquitous internet.

DK-CM,
Romford Market House,
Romford, London,
begun 2016

The Market House is a new civic and commercial building in the heart of Romford town centre, and part of a project to regenerate the area by Havering Council with the Mayor of London. The building has been designed as a timber-framed structure and will provide new market facilities and a spatial focus to the town centre.

DK-CM, Wroughton Academy,
Gorleston,
Great Yarmouth, Norfolk,
2018

DK-CM was commissioned to link two adjacent schools, one for infants and one for juniors, which now work as single entity. The design reworks the progressive language of the original junior school, which opened in 1950, in new materials to create a new 'front' to the whole site.

DK-CM,
Harrow Arts Centre,
Harrow, London,
2020

This project will create a new bookable community space and cultural facilities in formerly 'back of house' spaces at Harrow Arts Centre. It forms part of DK-CM's masterplan for the area, commissioned by Harrow Council.

South Cambridgeshire Village Design Guides,
Community engagement meeting for Caldecote
and Papworth Everard,
2018-19

Community engagement is a recurring part of DK-CM's work. In
this project for South Cambridgeshire District Council and parishes,
the practice worked with local residents to deliver adopted village
design guides to shape development in two village communities.

Building on this work, DK-CM have recently been writing design guidance for the future expansion of rural villages in South Cambridgeshire. We were able to design a methodology which acknowledged that future expansion was extremely likely and which enabled a public, villager-led conversation about the future of the settlement to take place. This was achieved by means of making a 'fanzine' with an editorial board of interested locals in the space of a day, drawing out annotated visual cues that together hinted at locally distinctive, progressive visions for the future of each village. The material collected in the fanzine was carefully recomposed into adoptable council design guidance, with the images and captions often surviving into the final adopted documents. In a way, we were taking the 'popular' approaches we find so inspiring from the late 20th century and plugging them directly into development management processes. In current work we find ourselves building on this method with a view to directly engaging with young people, 'future generations' and the wider nonhuman ecology of a place, for example in our Placemaking Study around the Grand Union Canal.

Unpicking some inheritances has allowed us to explore how DK-CM's work seeks to embody the commitment to public good of the postwar era whilst acknowledging and modifying its practices in response to the radical shifts in popular desire and public culture since that period. For the most part, these shifts are still to be fully recognised in architectural or planning practice, which continue to ask the public to 'participate' in the built environment professions when really it should be the professions that seek participation in the wider world. It is up to architects and planners to constantly adapt their own working methods to find relevance, meaning and agency in a messy, challenging world. ⌀

Notes
1. As cited in Colin Ward, *Welcome, Thinner City: Urban Survival in the 1990s*, Bedford Square Press (London), 1989, p.37.
2. Robert Venturi, Denise Scott Brown and Steven Izenour, *Learning from Las Vegas: The Forgotten Symbolism of Architectural Form*, The MIT Press (Cambridge, MA), 1977.
3. Tony Parker, *The People of Providence: A Housing Estate and Some of Its Inhabitants*, Hutchinson (London), 1983.
4. Mary Chamberlain, *Fenwomen: A Portrait of Women in an English Village*, Routledge & Kegan Paul (London), 1983.

DK-CM,
Canal Placemaking Study,
2018-19

Commissioned by the Old Oak and Park
Royal Development Corporation, this study
reimagines the Grand Union Canal as an
ecological corridor and site of environmental
education, getting the balance right between
occupation by people and wildlife.

The Joy of Architecture

Geoff Shearcroft

AOC,
V&A Museum of Childhood,
Bethnal Green,
London,
due for completion 2023

Redevelopment of a Victorian building to create
an essential contemporary museum for local
and international communities. The emotional
character of the space is defined by its content –
the colour, forms and materials of the collection
– and supported by the black-and-white
decoration of the regular cast-iron structure.

Evoking Emotions Through Building

Geoff Shearcroft – architect, architectural tutor, and director of London-based AOC Architecture – opines that joy is crucial in architecture and that this joy is not about adherence to styles or prescribed spatial protocols, but emotional engagement. Joy propagated Postmodernism in the 1970s and 1980s, and so today, in another economically unstable time, it is re-emerging, albeit differently.

To talk about joyfulness in an architectural school of 1965 was probably about as offbeat as discussing sex in a middle class parlour in 1865. Joy, for many, was simply not a serious property of architecture, if a property at all!
— Kent Bloomer on Charles Moore, 1986[1]

Then

Much postmodern architecture of the 1970s and 1980s is referred to as joyful, something that has been lacking from the desaturated materialist minimalism of the past twenty years. In a 1973 lecture at the Pratt Institute, the year before he died, the architect Louis Kahn declared, 'I think joy is the key word in our work. It must be felt.'[2] For Kahn joy was mystical and motivational, an impelling force that existed before us, that made us and that enabled us to create. So far, so Jedi. But joy enabled architects to create spaces 'that can talk and say something to you',[3] as distinct from the majority of architecture which was merely operational. Joyful architecture engaged people. It was not about fun, happiness or humour, it was about creating an emotional connection between the designed space and the human experience.

At the time when Kahn was publicly proclaiming the importance of joy to architects, *The Joy of Sex* was top of the *New York Times* bestseller list and the world was in the middle of the most significant stock market crash since the Great Depression. The UK economy did not recover to the same level until 1987, the US until 1993.[4] This violent decline in economic prosperity saw a radical realignment in popular politics, the dramatic rise of unemployment and the decline of government support for the health, happiness and fortunes of its citizens.

When Kahn died, joy was very much placed on the architectural agenda by his postmodern padawans, Charles Moore and Robert Venturi. Moore encouraged architects to look at places and listen to people, 'adding our own energies, care, and love, and even joy, if we have it in us'.[5] His joy was less mystical than Kahn's life force, more often found and recreated, celebrated and remembered, sampled and synthesised. Venturi's joy was more quotidian still. His iconoclastic 'Is not Main Street almost all right?'[6] brings Kahn's joy to ground. Venturi identified the personal joy he found in Mannerist architecture, from Michelangelo to the commercial strip, and dissected its forms in an attempt to create a useful lexicon and design strategies. This was a personal joy explained and given form.

May Day Fayre,
Chingford Plains,
Epping Forest,
London,
4 May 2019

A fleeting rainbow frames May Day's neo-pagan festivities, part of Waltham Forest's London Borough of Culture 2019. Rainbows are often associated with ecstatic joy, an occasional euphoria distinct from the habitual joy evoked by particular objects on a regular basis.

Venturi's and Moore's buildings, publications and teaching provided new tools for architects to respond to the new socio-economic order. The luxurious refinement of late Modernism could be replaced by simply rendered symbolism, expensive megastructures replaced by everyday decorated sheds. Colour, symbolism, sampling and decoration were used to rage against the machine, formally if not politically. The emphasis in architecture moved from what was right to what felt good. Truth was usurped by emotion, and the emotion pursued was joy.

Now

I like architecture that is joyful. I like buildings, experiences, places in which I find joy. As in 1965, joyfulness was not talked about when I was at architecture school in 1995. I discovered joyful architecture through visiting buildings. An unexpected recital by a young choir in the concrete clouds of Jørn Utzon's Bagsværd Church (Copenhagen, 1976) that ended as suddenly as it started. Sitting halfway up the stair in the Vanna Venturi House (Philadelphia, 1964), the sweet spot at the centre of an exploded domestic dream. Enjoying a rainbow framing neo-pagan towers at a May Day Fayre in Epping Forest, London. These were buildings that said something to me and demanded a response. This might best be described as ecstatic joy, a rare emotion provoked by the situation – the choir, our host's generosity, the brief rainbow – as much as the architecture itself.

Then there are buildings that bring me joy on a regular basis. The Hackney Empire, Tim Ronalds's

mash-up (2004) of Frank Matcham's Victorian theatre (1901), always brings me joy, lifting my mood as I cycle by. This is not the same as me liking the building or being trained to like the building. It evokes an unconscious emotional response, a habitual joy. Like the glow of the evening sun on the pink (Dulux Party Surprise 4) wall in my living room. Or the Aldo Rossi espresso pot I make coffee in every morning. These are intentional experiences of habitual joy that have been designed.

At AOC we describe our work as useful, valuable and joyful, an evolution of Vitruvius's strength, usefulness and beauty and a less moralistic take on John Ruskin's 'joy, humility and usefulness'.[7] An increasing number of our contemporaries (including contributors to this publication) also refer to joy when describing their work. Why this apparent convergence on joy? The turn of the millennium saw an increasing interest in the economics of happiness, as living standards rose and people sought more than the wealth, power and fame they had been promised in the past. Fuzzy feelings overturned hard facts. Gwyneth Paltrow's goop replaced Gordon Gekko's greed. In 2018, Ingrid Fetell Lee's book *Joyful* challenged the notion of joy being intangible, a mystical force, and made the case for the universal aesthetics of joy.[8] It is easy to dismiss the generic nature of her 10 universals and her ingratiating self-help conclusions. Yet the book's subtitle, 'The surprising power of ordinary things to create extraordinary happiness', seems an earnest take on Venturi's call to find joy in the everyday. Joy revisited.

Colour

Ingrid Fetell Lee boldly states that 'the liveliest places and objects all have one thing in common: bright vivid colour'.[9] Working through my personal catalogue of joyful places and objects, this is clearly not an absolute truth. Yet the use of colour is often associated with attempts to design joyful places. Two temporary buildings on London's South Bank demonstrate different approaches. The Lift (AOC, 2008) used a multicoloured pattern to enrich a building for a festival amidst the grey concrete and white Portland stone of a mid-20th-century arts centre. Coloured by diverse authors within our chosen parameters and arranged for formal effect, the bright colours were printed onto an all-enveloping membrane to enrich a distinct formal figure with multiple associations. Colour was applied to create a multivalent alien, at home in a range of settings. Nearby, The Shed (Haworth Tompkins, 2013) created a vivid, vermillion monolith next to the National Theatre (Denys Lasdun, 1976). Clad in stained timber boards that replicated the scale and texture of its grey neighbour's formwork, it evoked joy through both the contrast with and complement to the original building. Colour was again applied, but the synthesis of the red stain with material and context relied on its particular setting for its emotional impact.

Both buildings are (relatively) dumb boxes, using colour, material and texture to manipulate a surface to create joyful effects. This approach was theorised and widely propagated by Venturi and Denise Scott Brown who consistently used colour in their designs. Although the bright colours of their later Children's Museum of Houston, Texas (1992) or their Stevenson Library at Bard College, New York (1993) shout out, the colours in their earlier work were generally more subtle. With the Lieb House (Venturi, Scott Brown & Associates, 1969), they applied a light grey, off-white horizontal datum to allow the shingle-clad building to resonate with the scale of its original neighbours and lemon yellow highlights to lift the emotional effect of the building. At The Green in Nunhead, London (AOC, 2016) we developed these tactics, combining material and applied colour to alter scale and emotion. Red bricks with matching mortar allow a small building to feel big, whilst the subtle colours of the patterned brickwork shadows soften the red monolith in response to its neighbours. A pastel-green painted porch provides an emotional uplift, the colour complementing the brick and breaking its homogeneity to ensure it stands out whilst fitting in.

AOC,
The Lift,
Southbank Centre,
London,
2008

A demountable performance and meeting space for the London International Festival of Theatre. The polychromatic pattern printed on the building's membrane encourages a diverse range of associations and emotions wherever it is sited.

Haworth Tompkins,
The Shed,
Southbank Centre,
London,
2013

A temporary extension to Denys Lasdun's National Theatre (1976). The timber cladding replicates the scale and texture of its permanent neighbour's board-marked concrete, whilst the intense red stain makes it pop and hum with the surroundings.

AOC,
The Green,
Nunhead,
London,
2016

A new community centre, part of the architects' redevelopment of Nunhead Green (2011–20). The colours of raw and painted materials are chosen to complement each other, establish a relationship with the existing buildings and evoke particular emotions.

Curation

Aldo Rossi consistently used colour in his drawings, products and buildings, in a manner that challenges the reductiveness of Ingrid Fetell Lee's joy in colourful places. Much of his work emotionally veers towards the sadness of the monument and the remembered city rather than the joy and celebration of the contemporary, using colour to evoke a diverse range of emotions. In one of his last built works, the Quartier Schützenstrasse in Berlin (1997), he used colour strategically in relation to its material, testing the relationship between artificiality and vividness. Colour, materials and forms are curated to create a generous assemblage in which existing and found elements have an equivalent significance to the new. Joy is created through reframing the experience of the existing buildings and memories of past plots, a generous position that sits well alongside the current environmental imperative to reuse rather than replace.

From 2015 until 2019 AOC worked at Somerset House, an 18th-century government building in central London, to transform former Inland Revenue offices into a contemporary arts centre. The limited economic resources of an independent public institution encouraged us to rely on paint and other surface linings to alter the emotional effects of the heavy masonry of the existing spaces. The primitive symbolism of a blue sky on the ceiling of a courtyard infill. The painted white and grey memories of previously knocked-through terraced houses dividing large rooms and long corridors. New floors lined with water-cut, terrazzo-patterned, coloured natural linoleum. The curated assemblage of colour, found fragments and artworks aims to evoke joyful emotions through sensory effects and remembered stories.

AOC,
Somerset House Studios,
Westminster,
London,
2019

The redevelopment of 18th-century government offices to create a contemporary arts centre in central London. The emotional character of the existing structures is manipulated through a curated assemblage of coloured surface linings, found fragments and art.

Aldo Rossi,
Quartier Schützenstrasse,
Berlin,
1997

Colour is applied strategically in relation to its material. Aluminium cladding is intensely bright green and red whilst stucco uses more muted yellow, terracotta and blues. Bricks are employed for their earthy tones whilst stone and zinc are used raw.

Content

Charles Moore actively sought to avoid a perfectible style, preferring instead to create structures that 'gather the energies of people and places'.[10] His joy was particular, not universal. At the Faculty Club, University of California Santa Barbara (1968), with William Turnbull Jr he created a distinct, spatially complex building with simple plastered forms animated internally by an assemblage of colour, supergraphics, architectural fragments and artworks. Much of the emotional impact of the spaces comes from the inclusion of cultural content within the architecture – the Spanish Colonial Revival style, a collegiate character, neon graphics and large landscape paintings. The design is not a total work of art which requires everything to be in its place, but a coherent collage of content, loose enough for visitors to claim the space as their own and for elements to be replaced.

At the V&A Museum of Childhood in London's Bethnal Green, AOC have been briefed to create 'the most joyful museum in the world'. Bombast aside, we have sought to establish an uplifting emotional tone in a gloomy Victorian shed. Collaboration with curators and communities has allowed cultural content and social desires to inform the emotional effects.

MLTW (Charles Moore and William Turnbull Jr),
Faculty Club,
University of California,
Santa Barbara,
1968

A public building that seeks to gather the cultural content of a particular place and community. The 2016 restoration of the space calms down the original colour palette but maintains a loose spatial composition of colour, supergraphics, neon and art that invites engagement.

The collection is used to animate the architecture, its variety of forms, scales and arrangement in tension with the repetitive rhythm and central symmetry of the existing cast-iron structure. The black-and-white contrast of the 19th-century mosaic floor is continued up the columns with a painted helix of stripes, creating a distinct frame in which the polychromatic collage of collection and supergraphics can be enjoyed. Colour and content are curated to create a complex and inclusive assemblage in which joy is conceived as dynamic and evolutionary.

Agenda

Now, as then, joyful architecture evokes a positive, uplifting emotional response through its physical presence; occasionally ecstatic, more often habitual. It is not a style, brand or formal language. During the global recession of the 1970s joy provided the motivation, approach and tangible effects for many architects to positively engage with constrained resources. As the 2020s open with another period of global economic and socio-political volatility, joy has returned to the architectural agenda, evolving new strategies to create emotionally engaging buildings that, perhaps, might help us feel better. ⌐

Notes
1. Eugene J Johnson (ed), *Charles Moore: Buildings and Projects 1949–1986*, Rizzoli (New York), 1986, p 21.
2. Louis I Kahn, *1973: Brooklyn, New York* (Perspecta vol 19), The MIT Press (New York), 1982, p 100.
3. *Ibid*, p 100.
4. Philip E Davis, 'Comparing Bear Markets – 1973 and 2000', *National Institute Economic Review*, 183 (1), 1 January 2003, pp 78–89.
5. Johnson, *op cit*, pp 15–16.
6. Robert Venturi, *Complexity and Contradiction in Architecture*, Museum of Modern Art (New York), 2nd edition, 1977, p 104.
7. John Ruskin, *A Joy For Ever (And Its Price in the Market)*, George Allen (London), 1904, point 168.
8. Ingrid Fetell Lee, *Joyful: The Surprising Power of Ordinary Things to Create Extraordinary Happiness*, Rider (London), 2018.
9. *Ibid*, p 16.
10. Johnson, *op cit*, p 15.

Joy has returned to the architectural agenda, evolving new strategies to create emotionally engaging buildings that, perhaps, might help us feel better.

Remembering **in** Colour

In Conversation **with Artist/Designer** Yinka Ilori

Co-Guest-Editor of this ⵧ **Erin McKellar** interviews multidisciplinary artist/designer **Yinka Ilori** and discovers that behind his arresting patterned work of bold bright colours are his Nigerian-British heritage and a yearning to experience as much of human cultures as possible. This expansive embracing of cultural difference and its joys is facilitated by Ilori's imperative to collaborate inclusively.

Visitors to London's Dulwich Picture Gallery over summer 2019 encountered something rather different to the polite brick houses and picket fences of this leafy suburb of South London. Standing in front of Sir John Soane's famous gallery was the Colour Palace, a geometrically patterned pavilion designed by Yinka Ilori (pictured on the previous spread, inside the structure) and Pricegore architects. Reminiscent of boldly printed Nigerian Dutch wax fabric, the pavilion was free to all and played host to the rich social activities that so many London-area cultural institutions hold during the summer months. Intimate on the interior and brightly patterned on the exterior, the Colour Palace in many ways spoke to the approach of Ilori as a designer: he defines as a multidisciplinary artist who is inspired by travel and his British-Nigerian heritage to create work that is joyful, pleasurable and above all for everyone.

Being a multidisciplinary artist means that Ilori works to free himself from limitations. His London-based studio takes on projects ranging from architecture to textile design and, as a result, has the flexibility to work fluidly within various fields. He explains that the 'beauty' of this approach comes from not 'pigeon-holing yourself into one area of art and design', which can hinder your practice or growth. Indeed, he continues to learn and grow through each new project that Yinka Ilori Studio takes on, because each brief offers 'a different way in terms of my aesthetic, how I think about my design, my ideas, my visions', and he believes that it is this constant desire to evolve that sets him apart from other designers.

Yinka Ilori and
Pricegore architects,
The Colour Palace,
Dulwich Picture Gallery,
London,
2019

An element of childlike curiosity inspired Ilori's approach to the Colour Palace: 'When you're a young kid, you'll always remember something you've seen that's outstanding or mind-blowing. You'll tell everyone. And I wanted to evoke that child in every adult.'

Reminiscent of boldly printed Nigerian Dutch wax fabric, the pavilion was free to all and played host to the rich social activities that so many London-area cultural institutions hold during the summer months

Yinka Ilori,
Happy Street,
Thessaly Road Railway Bridge,
London,
2019

Ilori wanted to create work that celebrates
culture and multiculturalism and is inclusive:
'There's no "you can't come here because
you're this, or you're black, white or Asian".
It doesn't matter. Art is for everyone.'

Learning

Collaboration is an integral part of Ilori's process because in teaming up with architects, designers, contractors, engineers and so on 'we learn, and I learn'. Working on Happy Street (2019), a competition to revitalise the 'gloomy underpass' of the Thessaly Road Railway Bridge in Wandsworth, London, he learned to think more architecturally than ever before by partnering with engineers, the local council, National Rail and Red Deer architects. This process continued with the Colour Palace, on which he collaborated closely with Alex Gore and Dingle Price of Pricegore architects, with both studios ultimately emerging from the project having learned about each other's heritages and practices. According to Ilori, 'that's the beauty of collaboration – you get to share ideas and come into my world, and I get to go into their world. I always really hope that this will get other architects, designers and creatives to share culture and learn about culture because it's something that's very special.'

Learning about the world through travel has also been 'a huge part' of Ilori's design sourcebook; he returns from each trip with new inspiration. For him, travel means trying to understand: 'How do people in different countries interact with architecture? How do they interact with colour? What languages do they speak? How do they perform in intimate spaces? How do they walk? All those small things that I think we sometimes take for granted are the things that I really care about.' Even on short trips, Ilori immerses himself, even if only for an hour or so, into the local culture so that he can keep creating new narratives and telling new stories. This means that when he sets to work on a new project he is drawing from a wealth of cultures in a way that reflects the world today.

According to Ilori, 'that's the beauty of collaboration – you get to share ideas and come into my world, and I get to go into their world. I always really hope that this will get other architects, designers and creatives to share culture and learn about culture because it's something that's very special'

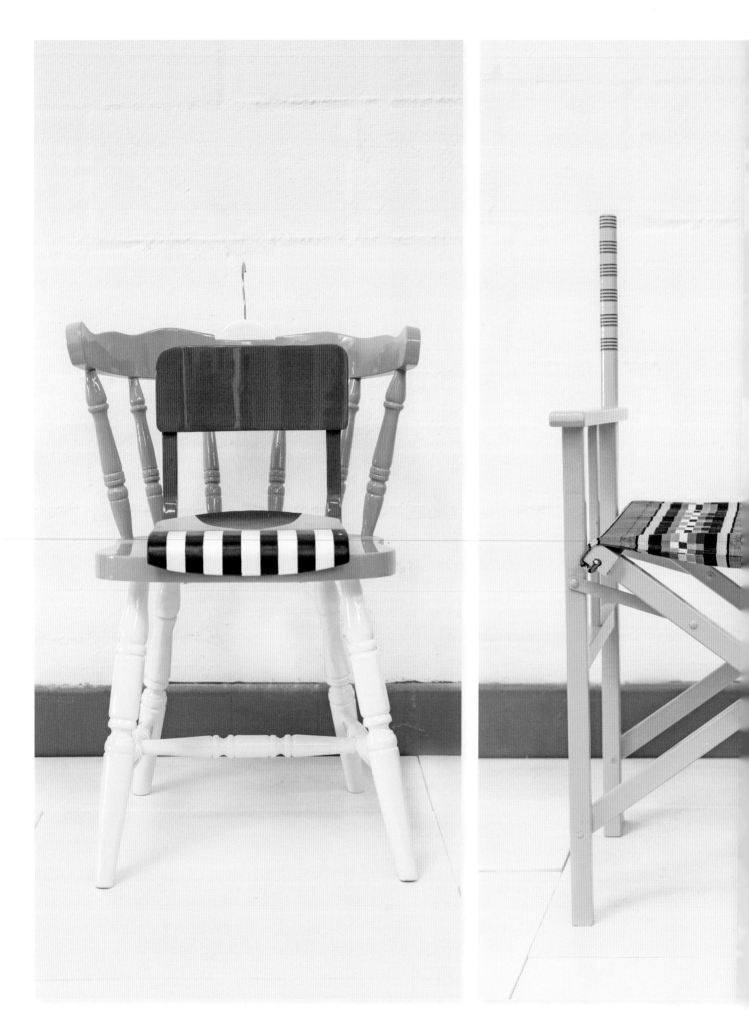

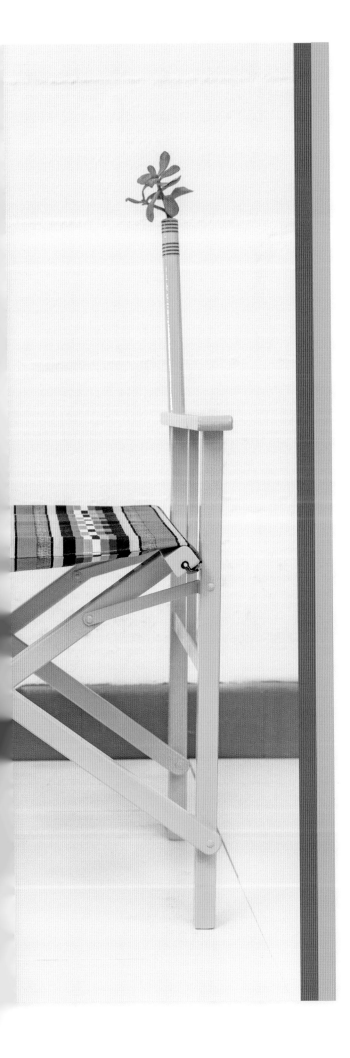

Culture

Part of what has helped Ilori come to an understanding of what 'culture' means has been his identity as a British-Nigerian designer. He feels very fortunate to have two cultures as this has enabled him to draw from both the amazing multiculturalism of his upbringing in North London and the rich craftsmanship and lively community spirit of Lagos. Throughout his childhood, his parents 'painted a picture' for him of Nigeria, into which he immersed himself fully. He first visited Lagos at the age of 11 or 12, and explains that this was when he first understood what culture is and what that culture meant to 'a nation that was full of energy and life and jubilance'. Since then he has continued to visit Nigeria and to integrate its narratives into his work and everyday life: 'I always discover new things about my culture and its history, for example even understanding that different fabrics mean different things to people in different cities.'

Ilori has absorbed various elements of Nigerian culture into his projects, expressing love of community, craftsmanship, colour and pattern. Originally trained in furniture design, his body of upcycled chairs – among them *A Trapped Star* and *Flower Bomb* (both 2015) – take the chairs from the charity shop to the gallery. He explains: 'I've always seen chairs as more than objects, rather as people, and as a result chairs tell stories.' Because chairs have always been with us in our homes, we all have a connection to them. In this way they can be seen as a constant, and as vessels of memory. Ilori's chairs retain their original narratives – their past uses – but are imbued with new meaning that reflects his identity. Though very Western, the original chairs had travelled into the homes of Londoners from diverse backgrounds, and as such Ilori considers the chairs to be 'immigrants'. 'Everyone's got this idea that they belong here or they belong there,' he insists, 'but in all honesty we are all immigrants. We're all travellers, we've all got roots.'

Yinka Ilori,
A Trapped Star,
2015

opposite: For Ilori, the journey of chairs mirrors the journey of people: 'These chairs come from flea markets. They serve a purpose in your household, to give you comfort and to bring people together, whether it's around the table or around key celebratory moments, and that's quite powerful. Chairs are immigrants, people are immigrants, so you share that journey.'

Yinka Ilori,
Flower Bomb,
2015

left: Giving the chair a narrative is only part of the process: 'I also like leaving the chair in a gallery and watching how people interact with the work. I would stand back and watch what people were saying about it. They would try to break down its narrative in a way I never thought they would, so that for me is amazing and what I love about chairs.'

Inclusivity

The idea of design as memory also operates at the scale of the architecture in Ilori's practice – he seeks inspiration from episodes from his past to tell stories for today. For Happy Street he created a public artwork comprising 56 enamel panels covered in a bold, rainbow-coloured pattern reminiscent of fabric. The surface of the Colour Palace also expressed joy in the form of a bright pattern – in this case one that explicitly aimed to re-create the sensation of being in Lagos's open-air markets. Ilori describes these as like London's Portobello Market on a busy Saturday with 10 times the number of people, 40 degrees heat 'and everyone trying to sell you anything and trying to pull you in their shop'. The geometric patterns of the facade, made up of individual slats of wood, appear to undulate and billow like cloth in a market stall.

Yinka Ilori and
Pricegore architects,
The Colour Palace,
Dulwich Picture Gallery,
London,
2019

When designing the Colour Palace, Ilori was inspired by his experience of Balogun Market in Lagos: 'I took elements of colour and created this kaleidoscopic experience that makes the colours shift as you walk around it.'

In projects like Happy Street and the Colour Palace he wanted to provide communities with spaces that were engaging, inviting, inclusive and celebratory of culture

By creating the pavilion in this form, Ilori captured the sensory qualities that he experiences when he visits Balogun Market in Lagos with his family and transported these to Dulwich in a lively and inviting structure that people would be drawn into. Growing up on a council estate in North London, Ilori didn't always feel welcomed into such spaces. In projects like Happy Street and the Colour Palace he wanted to provide communities with spaces that were engaging, inviting, inclusive and celebratory of culture: 'I think there's so much power in public work. It makes you feel happier. It promotes joy.' To achieve this sense of inclusivity and joy in his public art projects, he consults with local communities. For Happy Street and the Colour Palace his studio asked local children and parents what colours made them happy. By using colour to recall memories, Ilori explains, 'I remember my journey and where I came from. It's important to me that I use my work to inspire the young kid who lives on the council estate today. They are the ones who are going to take architecture to the next level so we need to inspire them.' ⌀

This article is based on a Skype conversation between Erin McKellar and Yinka Ilori on 4 April 2020.

Yinka Ilori,
Happy Street,
Thessaly Road
Railway Bridge,
London,
2019

Talking to local children was an essential part of the design process of Happy Street, but Ilori felt this benefited the kids as well: 'There have been a huge number of youth clubs that have been shut down, and there's not a lot of things that young kids can do when these types of spaces are no longer available.'

Iconic Iconoclasm
David Connor

A Word from
◭ Editor Neil Spiller

**P-TCO (David Connor),
Marco Pirroni Flat,
London,
1985**

This drawing carefully
predicts the aesthetic of
the finished space and
introduces the beaked
Nosferatu character who
stares bleakly out of the
drawing's frame.

Picture London in the early 1970s, still trying to heave itself out of the postwar mire, with swathes of the city left for dead and the happy, chilled hippie, trendy youths of the late 1960s about to transition into nihilistic, angry punks, which themselves would quickly metamorphose into the narcissistic flamboyance of the New Romantics by the end of the decade. On the whole London was depressed and prurient, its social divide bigger than ever. However these blossoms of colour and controversy – though the exception rather than the rule – were setting precedents that would echo throughout fashion, music and popular culture for many years and still do.

Enter an art-school student from Birmingham into the rarefied atmosphere of the louche Royal College of Art (RCA). For architectural designer David Connor this was a great catalytic time. It was the start of a career that has taken him from associating with punk royalty and being interior designer to New Romantic idol Adam Ant, to architecting an iconic house in California's Napa Valley, working on Vivienne Westwood stores and on projects with Anish Kapoor, and designing the interior of the Atlantic Bar & Grill – a social nightspot just off London's Piccadilly Circus for those in the know – and much, much more.

Then, the RCA Master's in Interior Design was run by Sir Hugh and Lady Casson (architect Sir Hugh had been Director of Architecture of London's Festival of Britain of 1951). The RCA's students had a sense of free and easy expectation that they would become design leaders. For Connor, this sense of design privilege and the extensive RCA network was creatively life-affirming and empowering, if at times a bit daunting. In 1974, in his second year, the Cassons moved on and the replacement head was architect John Miller who latterly delivered RIBA accreditation for the course, which was subsequently renamed 'Environmental Design' and became much more architectural. So this combination of Casson's flag-carrying for the embryonic discipline of interior design, and Miller's white, clean and neat British Modernism, created a unique learning environment for the young Connor.

This entrance hall / dining area, inspired by German Expressionism, contorts spatial perception to create a vivacious and arresting space, never letting the viewer's eye rest.

Detritus Chic to Eccentric Camp

In 1976, Malcolm McLaren and Vivienne Westwood's small shop 'Sex' at 430 King's Road in London's Chelsea needed a new design. The shop was rebranded as 'Seditionaries' and was to be the place from which punk emerged. Connor was introduced to McLaren and Westwood by fellow RCA graduate Ben Kelly. After developing some design ideas together, Kelly bowed out and Connor took on the design duties, working closely particularly with Westwood. The interior included a collage made by Connor of bomb-damaged Dresden. The shop became a mecca for aspiring anarchic punks. Connor's contribution was rewarded with the princely sum of £30 and 'a full set of [Westwood's] clothes. My mother threw them away later because the shirt had a swastika on it. I saw in a newspaper, recently, that they would be worth around £50K.'[1]

By 1979, McLaren and Westwood needed again to transform their small shop, to cater for the new breed of New Romantics, and called it 'World's End'. Again Connor was enlisted, this time to help tease out a new vision for the facade, which includes the now-iconic clock that runs backwards.

Connor established a partnership with fellow RCA graduate Julian Powell-Tuck in 1978. In 1982 they were joined by architect Gunnar Orefelt and became Powell-Tuck, Connor & Orefelt (P-TCO). McLaren's impresario duties expanded to more than managing the Sex Pistols and included New Romantic acts such as Bow Wow Wow and Adam and the Ants. Connor was asked to design an apartment for Adam Ant. For this commission, with P-TCO he took a rather scenographic approach. The use of much drapery, slightly overscaled furniture and a marbled ubiquitous painted surface on all walls and furniture gave the design a theatrical, slightly surreal feel – a set for Ant to stand and deliver his New Romantic lifestyle.

Ant's songwriting collaborator and guitarist, Marco Pirroni, also benefited from a small, extraordinary interior hallway/dining room

authored by Connor. 'Around 1982, Marco said he wanted something different. When I showed him the drawings he said, "not that different". The project came to fruition in 1985. The scheme is much more architecturally anarchic and punky than the more postmodern, classical Ant flat. Canted architraves, dados, skirtings and nonorthogonal doors all contribute to an otherworldly space that messes with the staid rules of human spatial perception – perspectives are contorted. Once more paint is called into Connor's service to blur the distinctions between wall, floor and architectural features and furniture, but here paint is paint and is not trying to fool the eye into thinking it is marble. However, the inspiration for the design is not to be found in the tatty, gob-encrusted irreverence of punk but of a much older movement: 'I always loved German Expressionist painting and cinema.' Connor had also taken to animating his drawings with strange

P-TCO (David Connor), Villa Zapu, Napa Valley, California, 1988

Connor's expressionistic drawing style is brought to bear on his proposal for a Modernist villa set alongside a vineyard – his most ambitious project up until that date.

The front of the house seen from its meandering approach pathway, showing the villa's striking appearance and its relationship with the landscape.

The guest tower seen from the rear of the main house across the swimming pool. The tower provides commanding views of the surrounding countryside, and its form and giant banners have provided the logo for the vineyard's wine labels.

bird-like human characters with angular shoulder pads, pushed-back or fallen-over chairs and spilt wine. Here at the Pirroni flat one of the crucial design drawings is populated with a bird-like figure, staring out at us, which interior design writer Drew Plunkett has attributed to a reference to the vampire from one of the greatest and most influential German Expressionistic films, FW Murnau's *Nosferatu* (1922).[2] The audaciously brilliant cacophony of Pirroni's space can be seen as a microcosm of much that was happening in the early to mid-1980s in London, at the Architectural Association, in furniture design, art and graphic design, condensed into a unruly, powerful decor.

Villa Zapu: A Heady Mix

In 1982 P-TCO was approach by a Swedish client who had bought a 130-acre (50-hectare) site in California's Napa Valley and intended to establish a new vineyard and build a house on top of a hill overlooking the site. It was Connor's first fully architectural project. 'In many ways I was too young to do this project, there were too many ideas in it.' To date, he had not built from new or structurally altered the projects he had worked on. This was virgin territory but clearly an opportunity not to be missed. For this project Connor reinvented his design persona again. Gone are traces of punk and New Romanticism, replaced by a gleaming white three-storey Modernist villa. The house was an original take on the spatial tactics, materiality and protocols of Modernism. This is no reworking of the tired dogmas of a movement then approaching three-quarters of a century old.

131

The final built project is an interplay between four formal architectural set pieces – the villa itself, the guest tower, a lengthy swimming pool between them, and the setting of these three elements in the landscape.

Connor's signature drawing style explored the external and internal spaces of the design: 'the very first drawings were best, where you swam from the main house to the guest tower'. His drawings are again peopled by the clients / Nosferatu / angular bird-like characters; sometimes a breast or nipple is glimpsed to add a soupcon of sexual frisson.

The anatomy of the house is one of a delicate balance between grandeur, domesticity and performative theatricality. It is modern yet has learnt from a variety of previous eras: there is something Egyptian about bits of it, something Art Deco about other bits and something of Deconstructivism in the way its wings twist and come to a point. No Le Corbusier-style ribbon windows here; windows are holes cut into thick walls framing views both to the outside but equally to the inside.

The performative preoccupations of the house, its client and its architect are perhaps best understood by viewing *Villa Zapu – A Short Film About a House* (1988).[3] On the one hand the house is a confrontation to the clients, forcing them to find new ways to inhabit it; on the other hand it is the backdrop for extravagant living, parties and posing choreographed around Connor's inimitable architectural set pieces, surprises and vignettes mixed with stark, ever-changing shadows and sunlight.

The simple device of Connor and others, in the film, donning the bird-like masks that so often feature in Connor's drawings effectively adds theatricality to the film and collapses its narrative space into a hybrid drawing/performance (not without uncanny-ness) which gets over the multiple aspects of the house's benign but questioning presence.

Connor throughout his career has worked internationally in Europe, Asia, America and the Caribbean and has been author of some spectacular projects that all exhibit his trademark eccentric architectural joy. Unfortunately, for the sake of this article only a few projects can be mentioned. A recent award-winning one is the beautiful Croft Lodge Studio.

The Romance of Ruins

Croft Lodge Studio is situated in the Herefordshire countryside in England and is a collaboration between Connor and Kate Darby Architects; they started working on it in 2012. It is in the grounds of a listed property and therefore listed itself, and originally was a small cottage and stables. Its found architectural condition was completely dilapidated and much of the property had already collapsed. Vegetation had grown through it and various animals had taken up residence over the years, yet it could not be demolished and a new build constructed.

David Connor Design / Kate Darby Architects, Croft Lodge Studio, Bircher Common, Herefordshire, 2016

A view taken from the outside of the studio through a window showing the juxtaposition of the new and dilapidated interior.

The fireplace/oven with its Connor-made head in the upper alcove, and a cluster of maquettes/rehearsals for it in the old bread-oven space.

The audacious and ingenious solution was to encapsulate the ruin completely in a new corrugated skin, to create the studio but to retain everything, as found: birds' nests, torn hessian sacking, spiders' webs, everything. What results architecturally is an extraordinary little building, sleek and simple on the outside. On the inside, its success relies on the dramatic contrast between the old structure and the tasteful, minimalist detailing of the new envelope, its fixtures and fittings. In 2017 the project won the *Architects' Journal* small projects award. A small fascinating detail of the project is a sculptural head Connor made for an alcove in the oven/fireplace reminiscent of the figures so prevalent in his drawings, staring out into existential space.

Whatever Connor works on, he brings a fresh, iconoclastic approach to his architecture. Each project is different yet iconic. If this issue of Ⅾ is about architectural stylistic transition and eclecticism, then Connor deserves his place in it: he has those qualities in spades. Ⅾ

Notes
1. All quotes are from email correspondence between the author and David Connor in April 2020.
2. Drew Plunkett, *Provocations: The Work of David Connor*, Lund Humphries (London), 2020, p 38.
3. *Villa Zapu – A Short Film About a House*, 1988, www.youtube.com/watch?v=f9FMhMHJ8ao

CONTRIBUTORS

Mat Barnes is the Director of CAN, an architecture practice based in London which takes a collaborative approach, allowing for an adaptive design process responding to the specific nuances of each brief. He has an interest in creating idiosyncratic and striking projects underwritten by cultural and historical research, and believes that architecture can and should make the city a more joyful, inclusive and inspiring place to live and work. CAN won a Royal Institute of British Architects (RIBA) award in 2019 and has been a finalist in the AJ Small Projects Award for the last two years.

Jennifer Bonner is an Associate Professor of Architecture at Harvard University Graduate School of Design (GSD) in Cambridge, Massachusetts. She founded creative practice MALL (Mass Architectural Loopty Loops, or Maximum Arches with Limited Liability – an acronym with built-in flexibility) in 2009.

Graham Burn is a director of Studio MUTT, a UK-based architecture practice founded in 2017 with roots in Liverpool and London. The studio believes in engaging with the world as it exists – adopting referencing and sampling as design solutions to contemporary issues. He studied architecture at the University of Liverpool, Bartlett School of Architecture, University College London (UCL) and the Architectural Association (AA) in London, and before establishing Studio MUTT worked for the RIBA Stirling-Prize-winning practice Allford Hall Monaghan Morris (AHMM).

James Crawford is a director of Studio MUTT. The studio's exciting and innovative proposals have brought international media coverage and invited exhibitions from Milan to Mexico. He studied architecture at the University of Liverpool and Royal College of Art (RCA) in London, and previously worked for the RIBA Stirling-Prize-winning practice dRMM Architects. Alongside his work at Studio MUTT, he currently teaches at the Liverpool School of Architecture.

Mario Carpo is Reyner Banham Professor of Architectural Theory and History at the Bartlett School of Architecture, UCL, and Professor of Architectural Theory at the University of Applied Arts, Vienna. His research and publications focus on the relationship between architectural theory, cultural history, and the history of media and information technology. His *Architecture in the Age of Printing* (2001) has been translated into several languages. His most recent books are *The Second Digital Turn: Design Beyond Intelligence* (The MIT Press, 2017), *The Alphabet and the Algorithm,* a history of digital design theory (The MIT Press, 2011), and the △ Reader *The Digital Turn in Architecture, 1992–2012* (John Wiley & Sons, 2013).

Yinka Ilori is a London-based multidisciplinary artist who specialises in storytelling by fusing his British and Nigerian heritage to tell new stories in contemporary design. Humorous, provocative and fun, every project he creates tells a story. Bringing Nigerian verbal traditional into playful conversation with contemporary design, his work touches on various global themes that resonate with different audiences all over the world.

David Knight is an urban strategist, author and educator, and a co-founder of DK-CM. He has worked on ambitious strategic, urban design, placemaking and policy projects since 2004, and holds a PhD in the politics of planning knowledge. He is a tutor at the RCA School of Architecture.

David Kohn is a director of David Kohn Architects, a London-based practice established in 2007 working internationally on arts, education and residential projects. He studied architecture at the University of Cambridge and at Columbia University, New York, as a Fulbright Scholar. He taught at the Cass School of Art, Architecture and Design in London between 2003 and 2013, and was subsequently a visiting professor at KU Leuven, Belgium. He is currently a diploma tutor at the AA.

Hugh McEwen is a partner at Office S&M. He has lectured for the RIBA and the Architecture Foundation in London, written for *Building Design* and the *Architectural Review,* and taught at the Bartlett School of Architecture, UCL, alongside Catrina Stewart. His drawings have been exhibited at the Royal Academy of Arts, and he is a recipient of the 2019 *RIBA Journal* Rising Stars Award.

Cristina Monteiro is a RIBA chartered architect and a co-founder of DK-CM. Her practice is concerned with understanding that what one creates is part of many ongoing narratives and the complex history and ecology of a place. She has over 15 years' experience working with the public sector to deliver public value in challenging contexts, from brief-writing and masterplanning to detailed design and delivery.

Stephen Parnell is an architect, architectural historian and critic, and teaches at the School of Architecture, Planning and Landscape at Newcastle University where he researches postwar architecture and its media. He has been researching △ since 2007 and is still writing its biography.

Lera Samovich studied architecture at the Moscow Institute of Architecture and Moscow Architecture School. She has collaborated professionally with Bureau Alexander Brodsky, Asse Architects and Nowadays Office. In 2014 she joined fala atelier in Porto, Portugal. She is regularly invited as a teacher, guest critic or lecturer at institutions including the Iuav University of Venice, Polytechnic University of Milan, and Delft University of Technology (TU Delft) in the Netherlands. In 2019 she completed her postgraduate research 'Shifting Orders: Practices of Composition and Displacement in Architecture of Álvaro Siza' at the Faculty of Architecture in Porto (FAUP).

Geoff Shearcroft is an architect, teacher and co-founder of AOC. Established in 2005, the London-based practice's realised projects include Somerset House Studios, Nunhead Green, the Crafts Council Gallery and the Wellcome Reading Room. They are currently leading the transformation of the V&A's Museum of Childhood and designing a new cultural centre in Shinfield, Berkshire. He taught at the Cass School of Art, Architecture and Design from 2006 to 2016, was a visiting professor at Yale University in New Haven, Connecticut, and currently leads a master's design studio at the University of Westminster in London.

Dirk Somers studied architecture in Antwerp and Milan, and graduated in Urban and Environmental Planning at KU Leuven. In 1999 he was awarded Young Flemish Designer. Since 2003 he has taught architectural design at TU Delft, and since September 2011 has been design professor at Ghent University, Belgium. He is the founder and manager of Antwerp-based Bovenbouw Architectuur. The office's work has been exhibited around the globe, from Munich to São Paulo, and London to Montreal. In 2019 Bovenbouw held its first solo exhibition in Antwerp and published its first monography.

Neil Spiller is Editor of ⌀, and was previously Hawksmoor Chair of Architecture and Landscape and Deputy Pro Vice Chancellor at the University of Greenwich, London. Prior to this he was Vice Dean at the Bartlett School of Architecture, UCL. He has made an international reputation as an architect, designer, artist, teacher, writer and polemicist. He is the founding director of the Advanced Virtual and Technological Architecture Research (AVATAR) group, which continues to push the boundaries of architectural design and discourse in the face of the impact of 21st-century technologies. Its current preoccupations include augmented and mixed realities and other metamorphic technologies.

Catrina Stewart is an architect and partner at Office S&M. She graduated with distinction from the Bartlett School of Architecture, UCL. She has taught at the Bartlett, Oxford Brookes University and the University of Brighton in the UK. Her work has been widely published and exhibited. She has lectured at the Royal Academy of Arts, the V&A and University of Cambridge. Before co-founding Office S&M, she worked with State of Play Games on a handmade computer game called Lumino City that was awarded a BAFTA for 'Artistic Achievement' in 2015.

Léa-Catherine Szacka is an architectural historian, critic and researcher. She is a Senior Lecturer in Architectural Studies at the University of Manchester and visiting tutor at the Berlage Center for Advanced Studies at TU Delft. In 2018 she was guest professor at Harvard GSD (as part of the Rotterdam studio abroad). She is the author of *Exhibiting the Postmodern: The 1980 Venice Architecture Biennale* (Marsilio, 2016) and *Biennials/Triennials: Conversations on the Geography of Itinerant Display* (Columbia Books on Architecture and the City, 2019). She is also co-editor of *Mediated Messages: Periodicals, Exhibitions and the Shaping of Postmodern Architecture* (Bloomsbury, 2018) and *Concrete Oslo* (Torpedo, 2018).

Amin Taha began an independent studio in 2003, and incorporated Groupwork as an Employee Ownership Trust of which he currently sits as chairman. As well as running the design and detailing of projects, he has taught, written and lectured on architecture, sat on the RIBA National and International Awards Jury, and aids property-related research groups and funds.

Alexander Turner is a director of Studio MUTT. The studio draws inspiration and ideas from urban, historical and social analysis to create characterful projects that are unique and joyful. Alexander studied Architecture at the University of Liverpool and RCA. Before establishing Studio MUTT, he worked for the RIBA Stirling-Prize-winning practice AHMM, and at SolidSpace with developer/architect Roger Zogolovitch. He currently teaches at the Liverpool School of Architecture.

Camille Walala is an artist known for ambitious and large-scale interventions in public spaces from Mayfair to Mauritius. Born in France and based in East London, her work encompasses full-facade murals, immersive 3D installations, street art, interiors and set design – characterised by a fusion of bold colours and playful geometric patterns. Her increasingly ambitious roster of international projects have included collaborations with leading global brands, the creative direction of a new hotel concept, major installations for WantedDesign and the London Design Festival, and a growing number of charity and social artistic initiatives.

What is *Architectural Design*?

Founded in 1930, *Architectural Design* (△) is an influential and prestigious publication. It combines the currency and topicality of a newsstand journal with the rigour and production qualities of a book. With an almost unrivalled reputation worldwide, it is consistently at the forefront of cultural thought and design.

Issues of △ are edited either by the journal Editor, Neil Spiller, or by an invited Guest-Editor. Renowned for being at the leading edge of design and new technologies, △ also covers themes as diverse as architectural history, the environment, interior design, landscape architecture and urban design.

Provocative and pioneering, △ inspires theoretical, creative and technological advances. It questions the outcome of technical innovations as well as the far-reaching social, cultural and environmental challenges that present themselves today.

For further information on △, subscriptions and purchasing single issues see:

https://onlinelibrary.wiley.com/journal/15542769

How to Subscribe
With 6 issues a year, you can subscribe to △ (either print, online or through the △ App for iPad)

Institutional subscription
£346 / $646
print or online

Institutional subscription
£433 / $808
combined print and online

Personal-rate subscription
£146 / $229
print and iPad access

Student-rate subscription
£93 / $147
print only

△ App for iPad
6-issue subscription:
£44.99 / US$64.99
Individual issue:
£9.99 / US$13.99

To subscribe to print or online
E: cs-journals@wiley.com

Americas
E: cs-journals@wiley.com
T: +1 877 762 2974

Europe, Middle East and Africa
E: cs-journals@wiley.com
T: +44 (0) 1865 778315

Asia Pacific
E: cs-journals@wiley.com
T: +65 6511 8000

Japan (for Japanese speaking support)
E: cs-japan@wiley.com
T: +65 6511 8010

Visit our Online Customer Help
available in 7 languages at www.wileycustomerhelp.com/ask

Volume 90 No 1
ISBN 978 1119 540038

Volume 90 No 2
ISBN 978 1119 555094

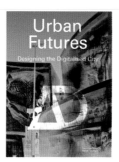

Volume 90 No 3
ISBN 978 1119 617563

Volume 90 No 4
ISBN 978 1119 576440

Volume 90 No 5
ISBN 978 1119 651581

Volume 90 No 6
ISBN 978 1119 685371